HOW TO IMPERSONATE FAMOUS PEOPLE

Your guidebook for
the ultimate alter-ego trip.

That's right,

HOW TO IMPERSONATE FAMOUS PEOPLE

will give you
easy step-by-step instructions
that will have you
walking and talking like your favorite star.

You'll dance like Fred Astaire,
wisecrack like Bette Davis,
prance like Rod Stewart,
humble yourself like Gandhi,
or put on your best Clint Eastwood
and tell your boss to make your day.

Remember, it's not who you are—
it's who you want to be.

HOW TO
IMPER

SONATE FAMOUS PEOPLE

Written by
CHRISTOPHER FOWLER

Illustrations by
STUART BUCKLEY

Prince Paperbacks
Crown Publishers, Inc.
New York

Text copyright © 1984 by Christopher Fowler
Illustrations copyright © 1984 by Stuart Buckley
A Prince Paperback Book

Published in the United States in 1985 by Crown
Publishers, Inc., One Park Avenue, New York, New
York 10016 and simultaneously in Canada by General
Publishing Company Limited

Originally published in Great Britain by Quartet Books
Limited, a member of the Namara Group, 27/
29 Goodge Street, London W1P 1FD

CROWN, PRINCE PAPERBACKS, and colophon are
trademarks of Crown Publishers, Inc.

Manufactured in the United States of America

Library of Congress Cataloging in Publication Data
Fowler, Christopher.
    How to impersonate famous people.

    (Prince paperbacks)
    1. Impersonation. 2. Entertainers—Anecdotes,
facetiae, satire, etc. 3. American wit and humor.
I. Title.
PN2071.I47F68 1985   792'.028'0207
85-11391
ISBN 0-517-55838-6

Cover and book design by Peter A. Davis

10 9 8 7 6 5 4 3 2 1

First American Edition

FOR KATH AND BILL

●●●●●●●●●●●●●●●

ACKNOWLEDGMENTS

Love and thanks to Jim "Pogs" Sturgeon, Sally "Fatlegs" Talbot, Brynn "Balloons" Lloyd and Simon, Roger "Woof" Smith and Bernard "Sanctions" Briquet, Kim "Too Tropical" Freitas, Maggie "Mrs. A" Armitage, Bee and Thurber Ottinger, David "Party Boy" Beckman, Larry "Fabulous" Evans, Boogaloo Sue, and Serafina.

ABOUT THE AUTHOR

Christopher Fowler is a charming, handsome, witty, and stylish young writer currently living in Hollywood, California. His hobbies include driving along Sunset Strip playing tropical dance music so loud it makes his ears sweat, smiling winningly at strangers in bars, and playing old Tony Hancock albums whenever it rains.

ABOUT THE ARTIST

Stuart Buckley is a charming, handsome, witty, and stylish young artist currently living near Regents Park, London. His hobbies include decorating his apartment in colors normally found only in discos...and the rest are still being checked out by the legal department.

CONTENTS

●●●●●●●●●●●●●●

THE ART OF
IMPERSONATION

●●●●●●●●●●●●●●●

What do you mean, you don't *do* impersonations? *Everyone* does impersonations!

The problem is, those people who think they have a natural flair for imitating celebrities rarely do.

Let's face it, anyone can knock out a passable imitation of W. C. Fields, but when was the last time you saw someone attempt to impersonate the Elephant Man? Anyone can muster up a passing resemblance to that old stand-by Mae West, but it takes a true *artiste* to carry off a decent Joan Crawford. Well, thanks to this crash course in faking the famous, you will be able to bring to life an impersonation of Shirley Temple that will be horrifyingly accurate to the original. You'll be able to wow 'em with a Rod Stewart so uncannily *apropos* it could land you in jail. Your performance as the divine Bette Midler could get you booked for a European summer tour.

With the aid of a few simple household props, a stack of mood-inducing records and a full-length mirror in which to practice, you can become a dozen of the world's most beloved celebrities in a matter of moments. Even if you're the sort of person who has yet to reach the conclusion of a joke and remember the punchline, you'll find all of these impersonations within your ability.

So why wait? Get to know the richest, most beautiful, beloved and famous people in the world from the *inside!* These are people who have more fun on a bad day than you have in your whole life. So you have nothing to lose. Let's be honest, you'll never be as rich and fabulous as the famous people in this book, but at least for a fleeting moment you can be just like them... and that's better than nothing, isn't it?

THATS THE MOST ABSHOID THING I EVER HOID -HIC

THE GROUND RULES OF
IMPERSONATION

●●●●●●●●●●●●●●●

We can't promise that your nifty impersonation of Babs Streisand singing "People" will help you on a dark night when confronted by an angry street gang, or that your moving rendition of "Heartbreak Hotel" in vintage Presley style will cause your bank manager to dismiss your enormous overdraft with a cheery tinkling laugh, but we *can* promise you a sort of spiritual purging, an uplifting sensation that can only be duplicated by pouring scouring powder into your underwear and riding your bicycle.

Impersonation is good for you. Remember, we're not trying for serious vocal mimicry, but something that combines the mannerisms of a famous person with your own magical personality to create something uniquely your own. This book will provide you with the blueprints of those mannerisms. What you add on top of them is up to you.

●●●●●●●●●●●●●●●

WHO ARE THE FAMOUS?

There exists a group of celebrities whose very names invite the most talentless party bore to drop into a pose and a catchphrase.

These are famous people who have become virtual parodies of themselves, thanks to years of being imitated by others.

"But hey," you ask, "if it's so easy to copy these people, how come I'm not making a squillion a year for appearing nightly on my own TV show?" Well, of course, the simple answer is that they thought of it first and have been getting away with being paid a fortune for just being themselves for years now.

Of course, you could take the mannerisms of half a dozen celebrities, mix and match 'em and create your own wonderful new superstar. We can't guarantee you'll get your own nightly TV show, but it should certainly produce looks of astounded horror when you surprise them with your new Garbo/Jagger combo impersonation, strutting around the room singing, "Hey you, I vant to be alone!"

Most of the impersonations we'll be doing are of showbiz personalities. The reason for this becomes apparent when you try to remember the last time you saw anyone do an impression of Dwight D. Eisenhower telling a joke. The majority of today's world leaders manage to be funny enough without you adding to them.

Remember, the more props you can get, the better. Most of these impersonations rely on physical actions—actions which increase in realism whenever you can get hold of the appropriate prop. That's why it is essential that you have a banana handy when doing Clint Eastwood (see pages 18—21).

Ready to begin? O.K., move back the furniture and send in the celebrities…

1

AL JOLSON

●●●●●●●●●●●●●●●●

We'll begin with an impersonation so simple that a child of three could manage it. And let's face it, who else would want to?

These days, Al Jolson, born Asa Yoelson, is remembered solely for his blackface performance of songs like "Mammy" and "Swanee River." Once America's most popular single entertainer, his legendary renditions moved audiences to tears. White audiences.

Today, more sophisticated audiences find Mr. Jolson's minstrel warblings breathtakingly offensive, so if you must include this in your repertoire, just be careful where you perform it.

If you are white, it's not a good idea to show this to a black person to prove that you are aware of his cultural heritage, especially at a party after a few drinks.

●●●●●●●●●●●●●●●●

PROPS REQUIRED

○ Black jacket
○ White gloves
○ Minstrel blackface (at your own risk)

●●●●●●●●●●●●●●●●

WHAT TO DO

① Drop on to one knee.
② Fling your arms out on either side.

③ As nasally as possible, sing the following:

"Mammy...
Mammy...
The sun shines east...
The sun shines west...
But I know where the sun shines best..."

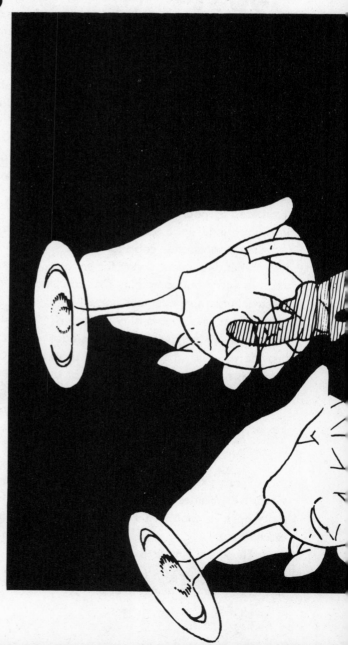

④ *"Way down upon the Swanee Riverrrrrr..."* may be substituted for the above. As you reach the end, twist the top half of your body back and forth, keeping your arms outstretched and still.

⑤ Bring your arms together, clasping your hands over your heart in a final tearful gesture.

⑥ Cut to a broad, sideways grin, pupils way off into the corners of the eyes.

⑦ Say: "You ain't heard nothin' yet, folks!"

⑧ Gauge audience reaction carefully and be prepared to leave the room as quickly as possible.

GROUCHO MARX

●●●●●●●●●●●●●●●

A popular favorite in bars and at parties, this one. You may care to throw it in as you hastily leave the room after your Al Jolson, particularly as it is one of the few impressions that can be performed on the run as well as standing still.

Sam and Minnie's son is probably the world's most popular impression, except in some parts of New Guinea, where the most popular impression is still that of a bush or small tree.

Every fancy-dress party has at least two Grouchos and a Harpo, and some even have a Chico. But nobody ever does an impression of Zeppo Marx, although this is the easiest of all.

You simply stand behind the rest, slightly to one side, as stiff as an ironing board (in fact you might try forcing one down the back of your jacket) bearing a bemused expression which says:

"Although I am the sensible one, I still appreciate the zany humor of my brothers." Groucho is much more fun.

●●●●●●●●●●●●●●●
PROPS REQUIRED

○ Two small oblong pieces of black card (eyebrows)
○ One larger oblong piece of black card (mustache)
○ Black ill-fitting dinner jacket
○ Joke plastic glasses with false nose attached
○ Large plastic squirt cigar

●●●●●●●●●●●●●●●
WHAT TO DO

① Loosen your jacket off your shoulders.
② Stoop forward.
③ Place one hand on the base of your spine, palm outwards.
④ Raise the other hand to your mouth, endlessly tapping your huge cigar. Keeping your little finger erect, tap with the two middle fingers.

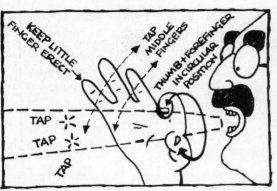

⑦ If anyone speaks, suddenly stand up straight and take a small, sharp step backward.

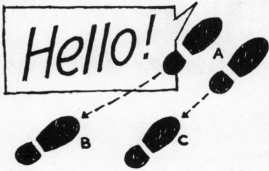

⑤ Look sideways and give a lecherous grin.

⑧ Say loudly:

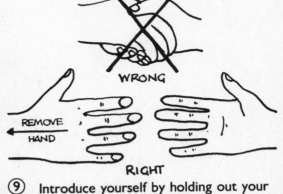

⑨ Introduce yourself by holding out your hand and saying: "We haven't met. My name is Otis B. Driftwood. My friends call me Otis—but you can call me anytime!"

⑩ When they hold out their hand to shake, remove your hand.

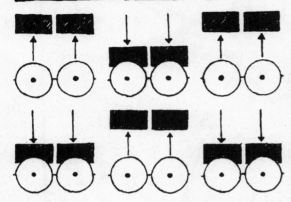

⑥ Raise eyebrows five or six times in quick succession.

5

HARPO MARX

●●●●●●●●●●●●●●●●

If you're good with props, this is the impersonation for you.

Obviously, the impression is a wordless one, and physical actions carry the whole thing off. Harpo allows you to be as crazy as you like and get away with it...up to a point. Hitting an elderly lady on the head

with a dead chicken, even when dressed as Harpo, is still frowned upon in some circles.

●●●●●●●●●●●●●●●●

PROPS REQUIRED

○ One overlength fawn raincoat (the bigger the better)

○ One long-stemmed bulb horn

○ One cheap yellow curly wig

○ One battered top hat

○ Absurd novelties to fill inner pockets of raincoat. For example:

○ A rubber chicken

○ A herring (if real, keep in plastic bag)

○ A large copper alarm clock, set to ring

○ A very long string of sausages—or colored handkerchiefs knotted together.

●●●●●●●●●●●●●●●●●●

WHAT TO DO

① Sidle up to the person of your choice, walking feet out and a little ahead of your body.

② Hands in your coat pockets, look from side to side in an exaggerated fashion.

③ Turn your head toward the person next to you and look him/her up and down very slowly.

④ Make classic Harpo face: cross eyes, puff out cheeks, and poke tip of tongue out.

⑤ Smile suddenly, and lower your head on to the person's shoulder. Look up at them with affection.

⑥ Suddenly bend your leg, grab the hands of the person next to you and place them on your thigh in a grip.

⑦ When they jump away, honk the bulb horn in your raincoat twice and produce herring/chicken/other.

⑧ Screw up eyes, slap thigh, double up in violent soundless laughter.

BETTE DAVIS

●●●●●●●●●●●●●

Everyone should know how to pass off a decent Bette Davis impersonation, if only in case of a sudden emergency. Indeed, in some circles a working knowledge of Ms. Davis's mannerisms is absolutely *de rigueur*, but I don't think we need to go into that.

●●●●●●●●●●●●●

EMERGENCY USE
OF BETTE DAVIS IMPERSONATION

Imagine the scene. Four or five of you are standing in a group at a social gathering. The talk has become so small it is in danger of vanishing altogether any second now. The man opposite looks as if he is about to tell you what made him choose accountancy as a profession. What should you do? Send for the Conversation Police? Ask the group if they know of a really good cure for herpes? Or launch into a memorable moment from Ms. Davis's long career? I leave the choice to you.

●●●●●●●●●●●●●

THE CLASSIC BETTE DAVIS
IMPERSONATION

① Shift your weight on to your left foot.
② Place your left hand on your left hip.
③ Raise your right arm so that the elbow touches your right hip.

④ Place a cigarette in your mouth. Straighten your index finger and forefinger, and remove cigarette with them, thumb pointing out.
⑤ Beginning at the mouth, swing the two fingers of your right hand sharply away in a semi-circle until your palm faces outward.
⑥ In as clipped a tone as possible, say the word "Peter." Pronounce it "Petah."

As soon as you have perfected the basic movement, graduate on to the following memorable Bette Davis lines.

●●●●●●●●●●●●●

CLASSIC BETTE DAVIS MOMENTS

LINE	DELIVERY
① "Did you know we have rats in the basement?"	Sing-song, sinister/ jolly
② "But you are a cripple, Blanche!"	Screaming, vindictive
③ "Fasten your seat belts…it's gonna be a bumpy night."	Swing shoulders suddenly toward person you are addressing
④ "Ha!"	Burst through door. Slam it shut. Fall back against it, throw head back and laugh
⑤ "Why…how dark it's gotten!"	Pathetic, searching the sky, eyes wide
⑥ "Would you mind moving? Body odor offends me."	Classic charming bitch attitude

Now name the films those lines came from (answers at the bottom of this page).

●●●●●●●●●●●●●●

ALL-PURPOSE
BETTE DAVIS GESTURE

Hold a cigarette between index finger and forefinger and place in mouth. *DO NOT TAKE HAND AWAY!* Look up at the person opposite you. Continue to stare up questioningly until person lights your cigarette. Once it is lit, tilt your head right back, never letting your eyes leave the other person's face. Take a huge noisy draw on cigarette as you do so. Hold for a second with head right back, then blow all of the smoke in the other person's face as hard as you can, looking at them with utter contempt.

The key to this impersonation is in the eyes. Try pretending that they are hard-boiled eggs. You need to achieve the effect of having eyes on stalks, like a snail. Practice makes perfect!

●●●●●●●●●●●●●●

BETTE AS BABY JANE;
PROPS REQUIRED

○ Old floral dress
○ Cheap blond wig
○ Silver tray with rat on it
○ Bowl of flour

To duplicate correctly the Baby Jane facial effect, just drop your head forward into the bowl of flour. Take it out and paint huge red lips and beauty spot on face. Try dancing on a crowded beach in this outfit, just like Bette. Watch how you suddenly get blanket space on even the most crowded stretches of sand.

Answers to Film Quotes *Whatever Happened to Baby Jane?* (1,2,4) *All About Eve* (3) *Dark Victory* (5) *The Anniversary* (6)

11

JAMES CAGNEY

●●●●●●●●●●●

Like Al Jolson, we are faced here with a famous person who has been imitated *ad infinitum* and always in the same manner. It's basically a combination of about three words and one gesture, and therefore remains an excellent impersonation for beginners.

Mr. Cagney is, of course, the definitive movie gangster, his fame resting chiefly on hard-boiled performances in films like *Public Enemy* and *White Heat.* He has, however, sung and danced, and in the Shakespearian field his magnificent Bottom is remarked upon to this day.

For this little performance you are not required to push a grapefruit—or anything else—into anyone's face.

●●●●●●●●●●●●●●●

THE BASIC CAGNEY IMPERSONATION

① Stand with your legs about two feet, six inches apart.

② Hold out your arms, keeping them well away from your body, hands resting on imaginary posts.

③ Bounce lightly up and down on the balls of your feet, at the same time moving the hands as if bouncing an imaginary basketball.

④ The immortal line must now be uttered in a breathy sing-song: "O.K. *(pause)* YOU *(pause)* DIRTY *(pause)* RATS *(pause)*

YOU'RE (pause) GONNA (pause) GET...IT ...NOW!"

Try slicking down your hair and letting one unruly forelock curl above your left eye.

CAGNEY DEATH SCENE

If for some reason you require to leave the room in a blaze of glory, try this:

① Imagine you are holding a machine gun by the strap in one hand.

② Rock back on heels, throw arms up wide.

③ Scream: *"MADE IT, MA! TOP OF THE WORLD!"*

④ Convincingly explode into a fiery inferno.

FRED GINGER
ASTAIRE & ROGERS

●●●●●●●●●●●●●●●●

Fred Austerlitz and Virginia McMath, more commonly known as Fred and Ginger, forever gave the impression that they were dancing on air. Well, the right clothes and the right music will soon make you feel you're dancing on air, although your downstairs neighbor will know that you're not.

To capture accurately the timeless *joie de vivre* of this enchanting couple, it is necessary to fling yourself about a bit, so during the trial run of this terpsichorean travesty it would be a good idea to wear sneakers.

Before placing your favorite album of thirties dance music on the stereo, it is essential to remove all breakables from the room. You'd be amazed how far the whip of a tailcoat can send a priceless piece of ceramic deco. What's more, you'll find that after a few sharp spins to the tune of "Let's Face the Music and Dance," your sense of balance will be put on "hold" long enough for you to attempt to enter the kitchen through the living room wall. In fact, your whirlwind finale could well surprise your partner enough to loosen his/her contact lenses, wind undergarments around the wrong way, and remove false teeth from the body like a champagne cork leaving a bottle.

Not only did the immortal Fred and Ginger manage to make this look effortless, they had the handicap of having to do it in black and white. If you want to increase the authenticity of your charade, a kitchen floor of black and white tiles can be helpful, providing your "lift and carry" movement doesn't deposit your partner in the sink.

The average living room can yield a variety of useful dance props. With a little imagination, that old couch can become an integral part of your performance as you *sproing* off it with arms and legs raised behind you. Back to back, arms raised like airplane wings, you spin around the dining room table and exit into the hall with your partner bent backward over your knee in a burst of loose feathers.

If you live near an old bandstand, you have the ultimate Fred and Ginger prop. ...It's roller skates on, wait for a thunderstorm and into a fast tap before the police get you.

Ultimately, a handful of Astaire-type gestures will pull you through any impersonation of the dazzling duo.

14

⚫⚫⚫⚫⚫⚫⚫⚫⚫⚫⚫⚫⚫

PROPS REQUIRED

◯ Tuxedo or tailcoat
◯ Evening gown
◯ Lightly molting feather boa

⚫⚫⚫⚫⚫⚫⚫⚫⚫⚫⚫⚫⚫

FOLLOWING IN FRED AND GINGER'S FOOTSTEPS

① THE BACK-TO-BACK AIRPLANE SPIN

This movement carries you in a wide circle at great speed and can be continued until one of you passes out. The end of the movement's "Drop-into-my-arms-and-I'll-catch-you" should be smooth and graceful. Allowing your partner to plunge to the floor like a felled tree can spoil an otherwise elegant moment and can seriously weaken the floor joists of your apartment.

As you spin back to back, remember to keep your toes tapping. Bottle caps attached to the soles make dandy tapshoes, but remember to remove the bottles first.

② THE SLOW LIFT

After a piece of fast tap, drop into "slow-motion-mode" as Fred entwines Ginger's waist with his arm, and with free hand outstretched raises her slowly in a smooth circling motion. Upon completion, Fred lowers his partner to the floor at a forty-five-degree angle *à la* Cyd Charisse in *Silk Stockings*.

Once again, the key element here is in not letting Ginger spin and thud to the floor in a flurry of feathers.

③ DUELING TAP SHOES

Roll back the carpet, face front a few feet apart from each other, and take turns to tap forward, raising your arms toward the end of the movement. Remain in the same place while your partner taps forward, then take your turn again, ending the

15

movement by grabbing your partner and leaping off in the direction of the sideboard in a sprawling waltz.

④ *GINGER ALONE*

While Fred and Ginger are standing apart, Ginger responds shyly to her partner's advances with eyes downcast, head turned away. Her arms from the elbow down are held horizontally at her waist with the palms of the hands at forty-five degrees. She moves the upper part of her body back and forth in little weaves, wafting hands in same movement a little later.

She finally succumbs and drops into...

⑤ *GRAND FLOURISH*

Even your most horribly clumsy, toe-stamping, face-bumping, spin-across-the-room-and-vanish-into-the-drapes errors can be forgiven and forgotten with a truly professional end flourish.

Fred faces his partner and takes her hands. Passing right through left, he raises his left arm high and slowly spins Ginger until her back faces the palm of his right hand.

Upon this, Ginger allows her body to fall back like a casually tossed overcoat over the arm of her partner. Depending on the flexibility of her spine and her partner's ability to catch a lot of weight at once, it is possible for her to touch the floor with the back of her right hand.

Note: Women weighing more than 196 pounds should give their partners plenty of warning (about three weeks, preferably in writing) if they plan to attempt this. This time will allow for the arrangement of mattresses, sandbags, scaffolding, etc.

The one movement common to all Fred and Ginger dances is of course the Spin, which Fred can do alone if he prefers,

dipping one arm as he does so; or you can do together, tapping and facing each other to break away every few seconds for just one full-turn spin before facing each other again.

● *A TIP*

In order to save wear and tear on the furniture, Fred may wish to paint a pair of sneakers black so that he may leap onto the sideboard for a quick spin without removing the veneer of the wood. Make sure any furniture to be leapt upon is pre–1955, as the woodwork of today is primarily constructed of chipboard and old crushed up record albums held together with staples and the same sort of glue that is used to seal the lids of cereal boxes.

BEST FRED AND GINGER DANCE MUSIC

① "Cheek to Cheek"
② "The Piccolino"
③ "Shall We Dance"
④ "Isn't This a Lovely Day (To Be Caught in the Rain)"

● *WARNING*

Never ever try this impression after more than three martinis, as many a drunken high kick has been known to remove wall hangings, implode TV picture tubes, and send the cat on a surprise aerial tour of the hallway.

CLINT
EASTWOOD

PROPS REQUIRED

- Flat-brimmed hat
- Piece of string
- Hall carpet
- Cheroot
- Table lamp

The Man with No Name is the perfect impersonation for the Person with No Talent, thanks to the wonderful world of props. Remembered primarily for his Italian cowboy epics and a couple of Dirty Harry movies, Clint is a character easily conjured and instantly recognizable. So let's see your version of a spaghetti shoot-out, as you gun down Lee Van Cleef to accompanying harmonica music.

Lee Van Cleef, by the way, may be impersonated exactly as Clint Eastwood, but with the eyes even narrower and the nostrils sucked right in.

WHAT TO DO

①   Lace string through flat brim of hat.

②   Cut circular hole in hall carpet and slip over head. (Perhaps you are lucky enough to have a fat sister. In which case, go through her wardrobe and find the Spanish poncho she used to wear in the seventies.)

③   Hang hat around back of neck. (If you choose to wear it on your head, make sure that the brim touches your eyebrows.)

④   Chew on cheroot by placing it in far corner of your mouth. If you do not smoke, you may use an eyebrow pencil. Be careful not to swallow it.

⑤   For what, you may ask, will we be using the table lamp? To which I answer, how else do we re-create the burning desert

sun? Take the shade off the lamp and stare into it for twenty minutes. This will produce the screwed-up facial appearance Clint bore in all of his horse operas.

⑥ Clench and bare teeth.

⑦ Screw eyes up to slits. (You should be getting sunspots by now anyway.)

⑧ Grunt a single word. It can be anything you like—the important thing is the tone. Test out a few to see which sounds the most surly. "Pyrex" has an insolent feel if pronounced correctly. So do "tulip" and "muffin." Having delivered your line, you may now leave the room.

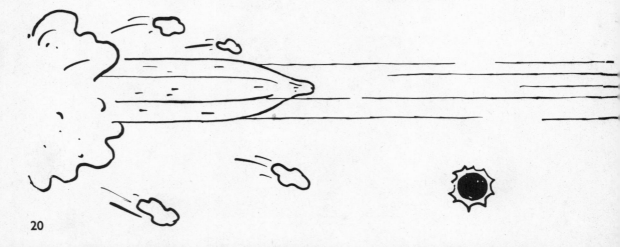

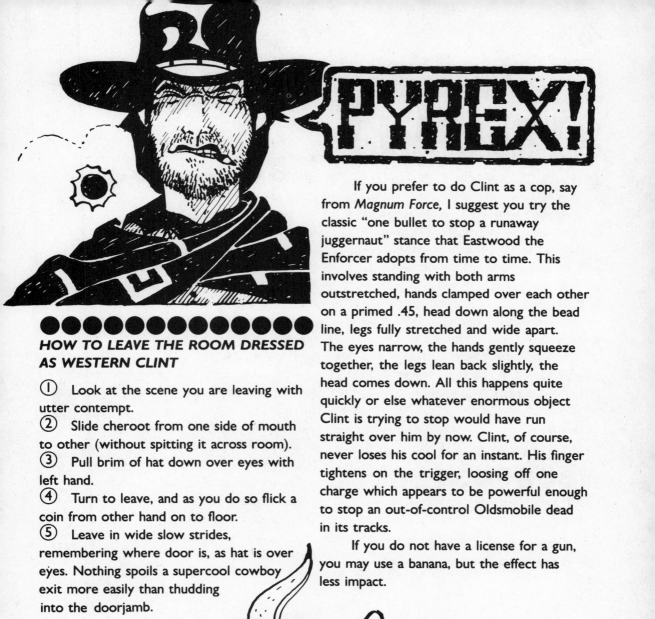

PYREX!

If you prefer to do Clint as a cop, say from *Magnum Force*, I suggest you try the classic "one bullet to stop a runaway juggernaut" stance that Eastwood the Enforcer adopts from time to time. This involves standing with both arms outstretched, hands clamped over each other on a primed .45, head down along the bead line, legs fully stretched and wide apart. The eyes narrow, the hands gently squeeze together, the legs lean back slightly, the head comes down. All this happens quite quickly or else whatever enormous object Clint is trying to stop would have run straight over him by now. Clint, of course, never loses his cool for an instant. His finger tightens on the trigger, loosing off one charge which appears to be powerful enough to stop an out-of-control Oldsmobile dead in its tracks.

If you do not have a license for a gun, you may use a banana, but the effect has less impact.

HOW TO LEAVE THE ROOM DRESSED AS WESTERN CLINT

①   Look at the scene you are leaving with utter contempt.

②   Slide cheroot from one side of mouth to other (without spitting it across room).

③   Pull brim of hat down over eyes with left hand.

④   Turn to leave, and as you do so flick a coin from other hand on to floor.

⑤   Leave in wide slow strides, remembering where door is, as hat is over eyes. Nothing spoils a supercool cowboy exit more easily than thudding into the doorjamb.

BARBRA STREISAND

●●●●●●●●●●●●●●●

Anyone who has a quarterly magazine devoted entirely to her lifestyle must be considered to be a superstar, and this ex-switchboard operator from Brooklyn is arguably the world's biggest.

The keynote in tackling such an awesome talent is to project dynamism in every little action. For the aid of such an impersonation, to achieve such charisma, one may be forced to resort to powerful drugs and painful surgical appliances. It just depends on how badly you wish to "do" an accurate Streisand.

●●●●●●●●●●●●●●●

PROPS REQUIRED

◯ Dish towel
◯ Copy of *Funny Girl* album
◯ Thousands of slavishly adoring fans (optional)

●●●●●●●●●●●●●●

WHAT TO DO

① Tie dish towel around your head.
② Put on the record at the "People" track.
③ Remain in profile the whole time.
④ As record starts, close eyes, draw deep breath and clasp hands to chest.

⑤ Attempt to extend your chin to the length of your nose.
⑥ Hunch shoulders up and forward. Begin singing.
⑦ Keep eyes closed. Look pained. Tilt head right back.
⑧ On long-held notes, keep changing the shape of your mouth, as if trying to find the right shape to fit the note.
⑨ On the word "luckiest" extend arms fully with hands turned right back.
⑩ Rotate hands with fingers splayed as far apart as possible. Effect should be as if hands are mounted on swivels and do not belong to the rest of your body. This movement is known as the "Shirley Bassey wrist-twist."
⑪ You may open your eyes from time to time, but *only* to look down your nose so that eyes are slightly crossed.
⑫ At climax of song, extend neck until as giraffe-like as possible and swivel head. Imagine you are washing soap off your face in the shower. Move mouth to widest possible setting for final long note. (There is *always* a final long note.)

On second thought, maybe you'd better just leave this to the lady. She does it well, and seems to enjoy it.

23

GANDHI

●●●●●●●●●●●●●●

Man of vision, bringer of peace, superstar of the eighties, the Mahatma finally made it with the youth market as the first movie star to get out of a sticky situation without using his fists.

This little brown pacifist was the E.T. of his time, the main difference being that he didn't vanish into a spaceship at the end. And for all his extraordinary struggles to bring peaceful equality to his nation, the Western world now remembers him through the movie version.

There's a lesson here, isn't there boys and girls?

●●●●●●●●●●●●●●●

PROPS REQUIRED

○ Chocolate brown bathing cap
○ Round rimless glasses

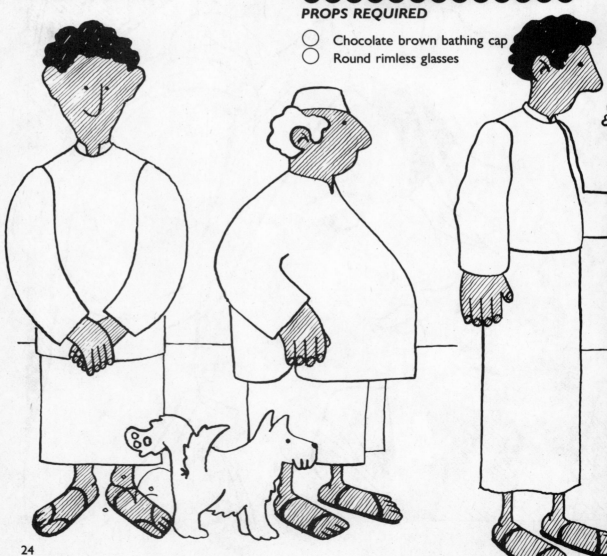

○ White sheet
○ Sandals
○ Stick
○ No more than a Prawn Biriani (Child's Portion) to eat in six months (optional)

●●●●●●●●●●●●●●●

WHAT TO DO

① Wrap naked self up in sheet.
② Don bathing cap.
③ Don specs and sandals.
④ Stand slightly bent at the stomach and lean on the stick.
⑤ Impersonate a small bird. Say, a sparrow or a wren. Peer about you in a delicate fashion.
⑥ Stride about purposefully before sitting on the floor crosslegged with hands clutching ankles.
⑦ Refuse a tray of canapes with a remark like: "Not a single pickle will pass my lips until my people are at peace."
⑧ Stay there long enough for everyone to get bored and ignore you.

POP

GANDHI

LINE FORMS HERE

LIZA
MINNELLI

●●●●●●●●●●●●●●●

Every party has at least two Sally Bowles outfits, normally picked by girls who mistakenly think they look good in black stockings. Like many other parodies, the best is done by Liza herself, and all with the aid of a chair and a bowler hat. All you have to remember with this one is to gush and giggle.

●●●●●●●●●●●●●●●●

PROPS REQUIRED

○ Copy of *Cabaret* album
○ Chair
○ Bowler hat
○ Suspenders
○ Eye shadow with sequins in it
○ Green nail polish
○ Arm-length gloves with fingers cut off

●●●●●●●●●●●●●●●●

WHAT TO DO

① Put on record of *Cabaret*. Get ready to gush.

② Make all movements sudden, sharp, and exaggerated; i.e., fling out your arms, twitch head, jerk shoulders, throw one hand high above head.

③ Suddenly raise right leg and stamp it onto chair (try not to go through it).

④ Now the tricky part: lean the weight of your torso onto your right leg and slide your left leg out behind you, slowly counterbalancing the weight of your body.

⑤ Place both hands on right kneecap and slowly bounce up and down. Gradually get faster and faster.

⑥ Just before you feel your achilles tendons snap, leap sideways onto chair to form Marlene Dietrich's famed V formation. This involves shaping your body like a V, with your hands on your knees and your torso leaning back.

⑦ Now with your right hand holding the chair back, use your left hand to lower bowler hat over eyes while making bicycle-pedaling movements with your legs.

⑧ As you do this, slowly straighten body out until head is right back and nearly touching floor.

⑨ After song has finished, gush, twitch, giggle, and brush hair out of eyes. Thank audience in breathy sobs. Repeatedly take a small sudden step forward, stop and turn sharply to other side of room.

⑩ For ballads, step forward on the long notes with arms outstretched behind you like a crashing dive bomber.

⑪ At end of song bend knees and raise one arm high above you, clutching your neck with the other hand as if trying to strangle yourself. (At this point you may not find it necessary to try and strangle yourself, as several people will offer to do it for you.)

NOËL COWARD

●●●●●●●●●●●●●●●●

An impersonation of Mr. Style himself will bring dignity to the roughest of evenings and may fool friends into thinking that you yourself possess wit, dignity, charm, etc. Then again, if you insist on doing Coward while clutching a can of beer and a bag of potato chips, maybe not.

It is important to have something to lean on when you remember that Noël and the other "children of the Ritz" hardly ever stood up straight. They were loungers, over pianos and against fireplaces, on bars and in deep armchairs. The overall effect is of seeing an extremely well-bred person who has had his spine surgically removed, and who only manages to stay leaning without collapsing into a jellied pool thanks to the amount of starch in his shirt.

●●●●●●●●●●●●●●●

PROPS REQUIRED

○ White dinner jacket
○ Red carnation
○ Cigarette holder
○ Black bow tie
○ Something to lean on

●●●●●●●●●●●●●●●

WHAT TO DO

① Place your left hand, flat and pointing downward, into your left jacket pocket. Try this wearing a silk dressing gown and cravat if you prefer.

② Hinge your right arm at the elbow and carelessly wave your cigarette holder. (Not too carelessly. One simply abhors the smell of burning party guests.)

③ Raise your eyebrows as high as they will go and arch them into an inverted V.

④ Lower your eyelids.

⑤ Look around you with your chin leading the rest of your face.

⑥ Speak from the back of your throat. The sound that emerges should resemble the early stages of a yawn. The whole art of speaking like Noël is in making every single word resemble the beginning of a yawn.

⑦ Now try a Coward catchphrase.

●●●●●●●●●●●●●●●●

ALL-PURPOSE NOËL COWARD CATCHPHRASES

"People's behavior away from Belgravia makes me aghast."

"One simply doesn't do Cap Ferrat any more."

"Very big, China."

"Don't be revolting, Millicent."

"I've a little man in Knightsbridge who does it for me."

All Noël Coward lines should be enunciated as if every word has a glass case over it. Speech must be clipped and clear. All "O" sounds must be pronounced as "Eaow," but they must not be drawn out.

●●●●●●●●●●●●●●●●

GOOD NOËL COWARD STANCES

Sitting up in bed reading the Sunday papers with a stack of pillows behind you.

Taking breakfast from a silver tray bearing a red rose in a slender vase.

Tapping a cigarette on the top of a silver cigarette case.

Sprawled across an ottoman in your dressing gown listening to Chopin.

●●●●●●●●●●●●●●●●

GOOD NOËL COWARD WORDS

"Frightful"   "Abominable"
"Ghastly"   "Unbearable"
"Horrid"   "Dreary"
"Beastly"

●●●●●●●●●●●●●●●●

GOOD OCCUPATIONS FOR A FEMALE NOËL COWARD CHARACTER

○ Coming in from the garden with a bunch of azaleas and saying "Did you call, Charles?"

○ Arranging said flowers in a porcelain vase for about two and a half hours.

○ Serving tea by holding the teapot high above the cup and touching the lid with the index finger of your left hand.

○ Offering around tiny platefuls of cucumber sandwiches with the crusts cut off.

○ Bursting noisily into tears.

○ Lying on the sofa looking languid.

○ Wasting away.

○ Standing on tiptoe looking out of the french windows with the right hand raised to shield the eyes.

○ Squeaking excitedly and fluttering the forearms back and forth near the face.

○ Coming in from the theater and saying "What an utterly ghastly night!" as you pull off your gloves.

○ For added realism to your impersonation, surround yourself with people who have nicknames like "Binky," "Pongo," "Biffo," and "Spotty."

LAUREL
& HARDY
●●●●●●●●●●●●●●●●●●

If Fred and Ginger got you into a fine mess, this comedy duo hailing from Lancashire, England, and Harlem, Georgia, respectively, should get you into another fine one. Fun and easy to do, Stan and Ollie have been popular impersonations since their films first appeared.

STAN LAUREL

① Stand with arms by sides, looking around the room slowly.

② With eyebrows raised as high as they will go, blink very slowly several times.

③ Still with eyebrows raised, smile with closed mouth and continue to blink slowly.

④ Raise left arm above head and lower hand to hair.

⑤ Scratch head as if squeezing a loaf of bread, allowing hand to bob up gently at the end of each squeeze.

OLIVER HARDY

① Look as fat as possible.

② Push lower part of face into neck to create treble-chinned "Liz Taylor" effect.

③ Look sheepish and embarrassed.

④ Swing top half of body back and forth from shoulders.

⑤ Look down at shoes sheepishly. Keep swinging body.

⑥ Look up without raising head as if you were a little boy who has just been scolded.

⑦ Try a tentative smile, then a grin. Fiddle with your tie. Twist the end of it around in knots.

⑧ Walk your fingers up a nearby doorframe and suddenly withdraw them with a "Hmmm Hmmm Hmmm."

OLLIE SAYS GOODBYE

① Blow little kisses using both hands, moving arms away like swinging gates.

② Make the last kiss a whopper. Giggle.

TOGETHER

Both give a little wave with the fingers, then turn and walk into the nearest wall.

STUNTS TO AVOID

○ Having housebricks bounce off your head with a *pok!* noise.

○ The Fourth-Floor-Upside-Down-Plunge-into-a-Rain-Barrel trick.

○ Lighting a cigarette with your thumb and forefinger.

○ The Legs-Away-from-Under-You-High-in-the-Air-and-Slam-onto-Your-Back Fall.

○ Running through a wall and into a cupboard full of crockery.

○ Any form of explosion which leaves you with tattered clothing, a sooty face, and a saucepan on your head.

○ Any attachment to a rope or pulley system which suddenly hoists you thirty feet into the air and bangs your head on a crossbeam.

○ Having household paint thrown into your face (minimum, one gallon).

○ Turning around and falling over a suitcase.

○ Sniffing the air for five minutes to work out that your bottom is on fire, with subsequent hurling of said bottom into horse trough.

○ Any driving of a vehicle which entails passing between two trains moving in opposite directions.

○ Sliding face-first down a shingle tiled roof into a vat of oatmeal-like substance.

REACTION TO STUNT

If you have to do a stunt, make it a custard-pie throwing. The official Laurel and Hardy society, "Sons of the Desert," are masters of this art.

The correct reaction to a pie in the face is to wipe one eye very slowly with the hand and wrist-flick the custard away, looking straight into the camera in an annoyed fashion. Slowly wipe the other eye free of custard and flick away. Then raise your head and drop it with a "Harrumph" in true Ollie style. If you find yourself teamed with a good partner, you'll be able to develop a ten-minute routine from merely trying to pass through a door together. Another good routine is the Laurel-and-Hardy-Panic, in which you run around each other howling, Ollie in a low "Oh-Oh-Oh-Oh-Oh" and Stan in a high whimpering squeal.

THE
ELEPHANT
MAN

●●●●●●●●●●●●●●

The best way to approach the Elephant Man is with your eyes shut, from a great distance. Be that as it may, he's a real partystopper, presuming you want your party stopped in the first place.

●●●●●●●●●●●●●●●●

PROPS REQUIRED

○ Sack with eyehole cut in it
○ Flesh-colored balloon
○ Two pairs of socks

●●●●●●●●●●●●●●●

WHAT TO DO

① Cut the end of the balloon off, fill with pairs of socks and pull over head.
② The lumpy side should be on the right side of your face, and the bigger the better, I say.
③ You may wish to hide the contents of your laundry basket down the shoulder of your shirt for added realism.
④ Remove your tie but keep the top button of your shirt done up.
⑤ Bend right knee, gnarl right hand inward, and lurch toward addressed party.
⑥ Open mouth on left side only (try taping right-hand side shut).

⑦ When you speak, breathe in as noisily as possible between sentences or parts of sentence. Ideally, you should be dragging back about half a pint of saliva each time, so that you sound like the tide drawing out on a pebbly beach.

⑧ Say the following: "I've never been treated schlschlschlrrrschlrrll so kindly before schlschlschlrrrlll Mr. Treves schlschlschrrll," etc. Give it plenty of mouth movement. Remember, you are trying hard to speak properly.

⑨ Lurch around suddenly and frighten small children to such an extent that they will wake up screaming in the night for weeks afterward.

⑩ Be pathetically grateful when somebody speaks to you. If someone offers to get you a drink, cry out, "How kind... schlschlschlrrllrrll...how very kind!"

You may prefer a more low-key approach to this one, in which case merely don the sack, put your overcoat on backward, and shuffle around the room staring at people through your eyehole. You may decide to "sock up" underneath the hood and arrange for someone to unmask you. It is wise to check your audience for anyone with a history of mental illness at this stage, as the overall effect of this one can be pretty disturbing.

Also, if you do plan a noisy unmasking scene and value your carpets, it might be an idea to have people set their drinks down or drink their cocktails from baby bottles.

MARLENE
DIETRICH
●●●●●●●●●●●●●●●

Those slothfully sinful eyes...the loitering, insolent walk...the trademarks the Berlin Bombshell are legend. Looking at Marlene one realizes the devil is truly a woman. For this piece of exotic sexual ambivalence you will need a chair.

PROPS REQUIRED

○ Top hat—preferably silver
○ Feather boa

Before your impersonation, arrange to have the room filled so full of cigarette smoke that one more Marlboro would set off the building sprinklers.

WHAT TO DO

① Put on any record you like. It doesn't make any difference—she never took any notice of what the orchestra was doing anyway.

② Talk through the music in a steady, flat tone.

③ Droop your eyelids until you can imagine them hanging down to your knees.

④ Lollop slowly around the room with your right hand pressed against your right thigh.

⑤ Move as if you were under water. Do everything extremely slowly.

⑥ In a sudden, fierce, erotically charged gesture, grab the back of your chair, lift it and slam it down.

⑦ Sit astride chair with the back in front of you. Place left hand on left knee, and grasping the chair back with your right hand lean back as far as you can.

⑧ Get up and sit sideways on chair. Cross right knee over left.

⑨ Place one hand on top of the other, fingers pinched together, and place both hands over your kneecaps.

⑩ Lean back until you form a perfect V. Gesture that song has ended by closing eyes entirely.

WARNING

If you are male and attempt this impersonation, you will look like:

① Helmut Berger in Visconti's *The Damned*

② Zaza Napoli in *La Cage Aux Folles II*.

Although of course this may be the effect you wish to achieve. I know better than to ask.

PETER SELLERS

As much a chameleon as a comedian, Peter Sellers allowed the screen characters he created to swallow his own personality. Nevertheless, he left us with a gallery of marvelous comic creations—the wheelchaired mad scientist from *Dr. Strangelove,* the uncomprehending Indian party guest from *The Party,* and of course the insanely incompetent French detective, Inspector Clouseau.

Our impersonation is taken from Mr. Sellers' most famous and repeated role—it's a fun, easy-to-do performance in which a little beforehand preparation helps turn every living room into a minefield of slapstick possibilities.

Remember, Inspector Clouseau is always right. He never admits to making a mistake. If something appears broken, Clouseau will insist on fixing it, even though all he does is make matters worse.

PROPS REQUIRED

◯ A baggy fawn raincoat
◯ An old fisherman's hat with turned-down brim
◯ Gloves
◯ A jar of cold cream
◯ A magnifying glass
◯ A telephone

WHAT TO DO

① Keep your hands thrust deep into your pockets. Be led into the room by a friend. When he turns a corner, you keep going. A few seconds later, reappear as if nothing had happened.

② Keeping your eyelids hooded and your eyes narrowed, survey the room by just moving your head.

③ Cross to the table and whip out your magnifying glass. Pick up the jar of cold cream. Unscrew the lid and peer into it.

④ Replace the lid, making sure you have left a blob of cream on the end of your nose. Leave it there for the rest of the impersonation.

⑤ Sit down on either a footstool or a backless sofa. Cross your legs and place your hands on top of each other over your knee. Keep your arms outstretched. Rock back and forth.

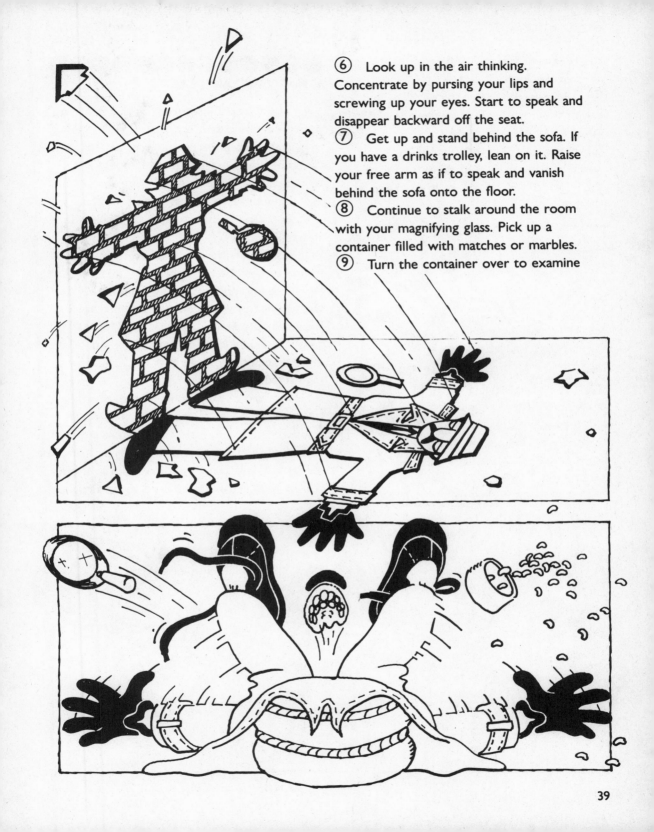

6 Look up in the air thinking. Concentrate by pursing your lips and screwing up your eyes. Start to speak and disappear backward off the seat.

7 Get up and stand behind the sofa. If you have a drinks trolley, lean on it. Raise your free arm as if to speak and vanish behind the sofa onto the floor.

8 Continue to stalk around the room with your magnifying glass. Pick up a container filled with matches or marbles.

9 Turn the container over to examine

the base and have everything inside fall out all over the table.

⑩ Pick up the telephone receiver and say to the host: "May I use the pheune?" After failing to hear a dial tone, unscrew the cap of the receiver and remove yards of wiring. Attempt to stuff the wiring back into the receiver and fail. Leave it in a heap on the table.

THE CLOUSEAU REACTION

The intrepid inspector has the ability to miss every important criminal event. He is so wrapped up in his own pomposity that a "beumb" could explode and he would fail to notice.

① Announce to the assembled guests: "I have reason to believe that the thief is in this reum."

② As you are saying this, have somebody noisily exit via the door behind you.

③ Keeping your arms by your side, turn the top half of your body halfway around and look behind you.

④ Now face front and say: "So I must insist that nobody leave until I complete my investigations."

A word of caution: over-enthusiasm in this role can lead to hospitalization. As an added touch, you may wish to have a Chinese friend leap out of the refrigerator and attack you, but don't leave him in there too long, as refrigerators tend to be airtight.

ROD STEWART

●●●●●●●●●●●●●●●●

That's right, rock stars are technically people too, so there's no excuse for avoiding this quick and easy impersonation of one of rock's greatest, er, greatest...whatevers. Famous more for being photographed with a variety of blond bimbos in airport departure lounges than for the memorability of his music, the spiky-headed singer is renowned for invoking one eternal question whenever his face appears in the tabloids. Namely: "What on earth does she see in him?"

●●●●●●●●●●●●●●
PROPS REQUIRED

- ○ One pair of *very* tight white trousers
- ○ Tartan scarf
- ○ Pillow
- ○ Hair spray
- ○ Comb
- ○ Microphone

●●●●●●●●●●●●●●
HOW TO PREPARE

First, take the pillow and scream into it for two days. When your voice has attained the resonance of a cheese grater being pulled across a sheet of sandpaper, you are ready.

Comb your hair starting from the front,

straight through to the back. Quickly put your head between your legs and apply hair spray, using as much as it would take to revarnish a painting the size of, say, Rembrandt's "The Night Watch." The tufts of your hair should be hard enough to punch a hole in a piece of Styrofoam. If not, spray hair again. Don't worry about the earth's ozone layer. It will regenerate.

Now don the tight white trousers. Keep breathing in until you can do up the top button. One simple way to tell if your trousers are tight enough: after you have removed them, the impression of the top button should remain imprinted on your stomach for no less than forty-eight hours.

Tie the tartan scarf around your neck. You may mime to "Atlantic Crossing" or "Every Picture Tells a Story" but the ideal song to play is "Do You Think I'm Sexy," as it allows more pout and pose per pulse.

It is important to remember that Rod rarely stands up straight while he is singing. He leans either very far forward, or with the top half of his body backward. Clutching your microphone, or similar-shaped object, place the record on the turntable and let's begin.

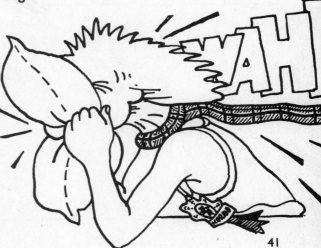

WHAT TO DO

① Bounce lightly up and down on the balls of your feet.

② As soon as chorus begins, pull mike close to mouth and scream hard, bending the top half of your body forward as you do so.

③ Now bend way back and let out a yell between lines.

④ Strut forward with one arm raised, bouncing as you go, lifting feet high.

⑤ Turn around and strut away with bottom sticking out.

⑥ Stop, stand with legs wide apart, and place free hand on hip.

⑦ Turn head around to look at audience over shoulder.

⑧ Spin around and strut back with head turned to one side, still screaming. Hand may remain on hip as long as you like.

⑨ Pout. Jerk head back and forth. Look pained. Sweat.

⑩ Gyrating pelvis back and forth, repeat the above. Stamp and flick microphone cord out of way. Take little jumps in the air with both feet off ground at same time.

⑪ Swing right arm above head and down, flick head with a flourish at end.

⑫ You may want to continue onward, but at a less forceful pace. Decrease strength

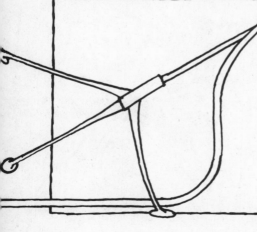

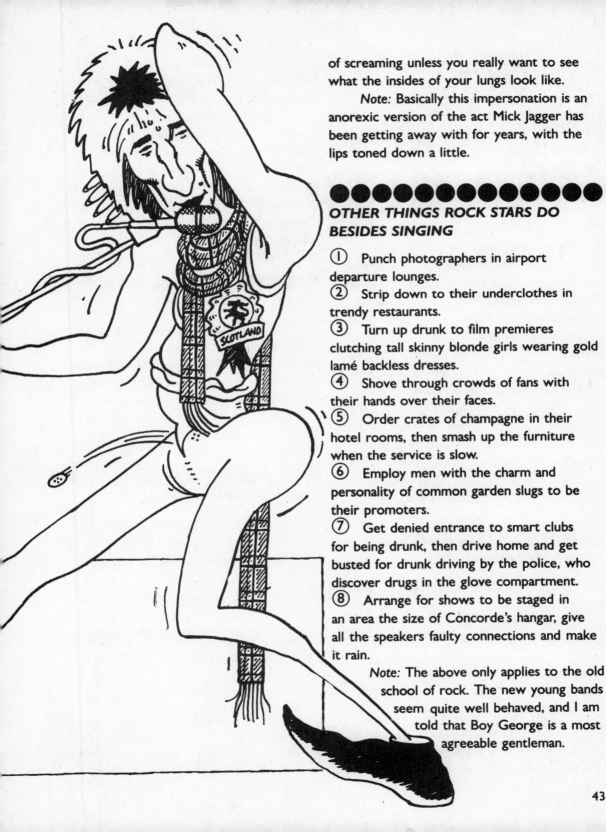

of screaming unless you really want to see what the insides of your lungs look like.

Note: Basically this impersonation is an anorexic version of the act Mick Jagger has been getting away with for years, with the lips toned down a little.

●●●●●●●●●●●●●●●

OTHER THINGS ROCK STARS DO BESIDES SINGING

① Punch photographers in airport departure lounges.

② Strip down to their underclothes in trendy restaurants.

③ Turn up drunk to film premieres clutching tall skinny blonde girls wearing gold lamé backless dresses.

④ Shove through crowds of fans with their hands over their faces.

⑤ Order crates of champagne in their hotel rooms, then smash up the furniture when the service is slow.

⑥ Employ men with the charm and personality of common garden slugs to be their promoters.

⑦ Get denied entrance to smart clubs for being drunk, then drive home and get busted for drunk driving by the police, who discover drugs in the glove compartment.

⑧ Arrange for shows to be staged in an area the size of Concorde's hangar, give all the speakers faulty connections and make it rain.

Note: The above only applies to the old school of rock. The new young bands seem quite well behaved, and I am told that Boy George is a most agreeable gentleman.

CARMEN MIRANDA

●●●●●●●●●●●●●●●●

Carmen Miranda, born Maria do Carmo Miranda da Cunha, was, you remember, the tiny Rio bombshell whose platform shoes and fruity headpieces added over a full foot to her height. The energetic star of movies like *Down Argentine Way* and *Copacabana* went through the same ritualized movements in just about all of the song-and-dance numbers she stamped her way through. Ah, the maracas, the bongos, the cries of "Chica Chica Boom Chic" that heralded the arrival of this big-nosed tiny-limbed South American songbird! How did she stay on those shoes? How did she balance those headdresses? Did she ever find anyone to spend a weekend with in Havana? Now *you* can provide an answer to these questions!

●●●●●●●●●●●●●●●●
PROPS REQUIRED

○ Bowl of plastic fruit (at least ten pieces, bananas essential)
○ Tube of glue
○ Dish towel (floral)
○ Old pair of stacked shoes from early seventies
○ Arm-length gloves
○ Frilly dress or bedspread
Note: These props are needed only if

you decide to go into this hammer and tongs. For your basic impression all you need is hands and feet.

The secret of a good Carmen Miranda is simple: the head *never* moves. It faces front, perhaps tilting a fraction, while the rest of the body does the work. The eyes swivel like runaway yoyos, the arms flail like a demented octopus...but the head stays immobile. There is a reason for this. You are wearing half a fruit stand.

●●●●●●●●●●●●●●●●
PREPARATION OF OUTFIT

Highly patterned dress or bedspread should be split to the waist. Glue all the pieces of plastic fruit on top of each other. Be creative. If the bowl is made of raffia, throw that in as well. Stick the whole lot to the dish towel and tie it around your head. Step into your stacks.

●●●●●●●●●●●●●●●●
IDEAL CARMEN MIRANDA MUSIC

① "I Yi Yi Yi Yi I Like You Very Much"
② "Weekend in Havana"
③ "South American Way"
④ "Co Co Co Co Co Ro"
⑤ "Chica Chica Boom Chic"

●●●●●●●●●●●●●●●●
ALL-PURPOSE MOVEMENT No. 1

① Bounce up and down to get into rhythm.
② Make "bicycling" motion with legs, lifting each alternately.

③ Take four steps forward.

④ Take four steps backward.

⑤ Roll arms over each other so that forearms are parallel, about a foot apart.

⑥ Make one complete "roll" of arms with each step.

⑦ *KEEP YOUR HEAD STILL!* Try to tilt and you'll go over like a felled tree.

⑧ Grin broadly.

⑨ Roll eyes right around the top of your head until you think they will drop out of their sockets.

⑩ Now involve your face in a smile so broad that it closes your eyes up completely.

●●●●●●●● ALL-PURPOSE MOVEMENT No. 2

① Perform leg movements as previously described.

② Place right forearm horizontally in front of your chest.

③ Place left forearm vertically so that left elbow touches right fist, forming an L.

④ Switch arms so that right elbow touches left fist in reverse L.

⑤ Change arms over on every second bounce.

●●●●●●●●●●● GOOD RUBBISH TO SING

You don't need samba music to do a good Carmen if you know these handy phrases. Just sing them repeatedly in any order. For variety why not toss in the odd line of poorly scanned pidgin Eengliss?

① I YiYiYiYiChica ChicaCoCoCoRioooo!

② Yoo Boya Boom La La Boom Bam Boo!

③ Yoya Oo La Layya Boom Boom Co Co Co Bam Boo Laya Lay!

And that's quite enough of that.

If you lack a pair of maracas, two painted baked bean cans filled with dried peas make an effective sound, if not an attractive appearance.

ELVIS PRESLEY

●●●●●●●●●●●●●

The Man. The Legend. The King. The Pelvis. And now, the Impersonation. Those wishing to clothe themselves in the garb of the late Memphis singer have two choices:

● *EARLY ELVIS*

Tight Levi's, denim shirt, slicked-down hair with unruly forelock, sneakers.

● *LATE ELVIS*

White studded jumpsuit with turned up collar, pillow down the front, wide studded belt, sideburns, sweat.

The rest of us will be content with arranging our bodies into four main Elvis-impression modes.

① *THE FACE*

The overriding Elvis facial feature was the Sneer. This involves wrinkling the nose so that a crease forms from the side of one nostril to the edge of the mouth. The eyelids droop slightly, the mouth sneers and the lips purse. Elvis had a small mouth, and by pursing the lips it was squeezed from his face until it looked about to fall on the floor.

② *THE ARMS*

Except for when they are touching a guitar, hands and arms remain above the head with the fingers clicking like a demented Spanish flamenco dancer.

③ *THE HIPS*

The keynote of any Elvis impression. It was the famous "Pelvic Thrust" movement which originally got Elvis into trouble and resulted in the cameramen on TV's Ed Sullivan show filming the singer from above the waist only. By today's standards it's hard to see what all the fuss was about, the movement being not so much a back-and-forth one as a grinding rotary gyration. Swivel your hips as if describing a full 360-degree circle.

④ *THE LEGS*

Imagine that, while one leg is barely able to support you and is in constant danger of giving way, the other is made entirely of rubber and will hold no weight at all. Keeping the left leg crooked, wiggle the right knee in and out as far as it will go. Try both legs at once, standing on the balls of your feet.

● *WARNING*

Don't try all of these movements at once or you will fall over.

The Elvis that people like to remember most existed in the period before he was drafted, leading up to the making of *Jailhouse Rock*. At that time he appeared dark and sexy, and just a little dangerous. The smouldering looks subsequently vanished in a welter of wholesome and bland beach movies. So grease back that hair, hang down that front forelock, pout, pucker, sneer, and loosen your joints—particularly the knees—before launching into:

BEST ELVIS MUSIC FOR IMPERSONATIONS

1. "Heartbreak Hotel"
2. "Hound Dog"
3. "Jailhouse Rock"
4. "Love Me Tender"
5. "You'll Never Walk Alone"

Note: If you are performing in the Early Elvis Mode, it is necessary to wear jeans which are about two feet too long so that you have really huge turn-ups. You should also be able to tuck a pack of cigarettes into the sleeve of your T-shirt without breaking them open and scattering tobacco all over you. If you think you look odd, take a look at how mid-seventies glitter rock looks now and be thankful for the fifties.

RUTH GORDON

●●●●●●●●●●●●●

Well, with the basics beneath your belt it might be fun to try an outsider at this stage. In this case, even if your impression is terrible they'll have to give you marks for the mere idea of impersonating a woman who was born in the previous century. Ruth Gordon's career as an actress and screenwriter has been nothing if not long and varied, but she is chiefly remembered now as the satanic neighbor in *Rosemary's Baby* and as Bud Cort's girlfriend in the cult classic *Harold and Maude*. It is from the latter that we derive a simple and definitive Ruth Gordon.

●●●●●●●●●●●●●

WHAT TO DO

① Take a bite into an orange and leave it in your mouth.
② Screw up your face thoughtfully.
③ Scratch the back of your head.

●●●●●●●●●●●●●

ALTERNATIVE No. 1

① Attract the attention of a friend by pressing your tongue against your teeth and going "Tsst."
② Nudge them and say: "Want some licorice?"

●●●●●●●●●●●●●

ALTERNATIVE No. 2

① Nudge a friend by giving them a glancing blow on the shoulder with the heel of your right hand.
② Say conspiratorially: "Get out there and live, otherwise you got nothing to talk about in the locker room!" End sentence with a hint of sexuality.
③ Wink and stick the tip of your tongue out between your teeth.

Serious imitators of Ms. Gordon will need to put their hair up in a bun and stick a pair of chopsticks in the back in order to look spritely and hip.

●●●●●●●●●●●●●

THE RUTH GORDON COMPLEXION

Problem: how to look over eighty simply and effectively? One friend suggests repeatedly hitting your face with a steak hammer until the skin loosens. Personally, I do not recommend this unless you have a foolproof way of tightening it back up again. Rubber cement may achieve a wrinkled, unsightly look upon drying, but the most convincing way of making your face appear ancient is by gluing pieces of corrugated cardboard to your cheeks and then pulling a balloon over your head (don't forget those breathing holes!). Cut the top off to allow your hair to stick through... better still, stick to impersonating Elvis Presley.

JOAN CRAWFORD

●●●●●●●●●●●●●●

O.K., so she never laid a finger on the kid. *Wink.* It's still very tempting to revise all impersonations of Ms. Crawford to make her into a monster, ever since Faye Dunaway chewed up the scenery in *Mommie Dearest.* But there were other sides to Lucille Fay LeSueur throughout the years of fame—all of them exactly the same, with the exception of a brief period when she was a platinum blonde!

Your version of Joan will sport a definitive look....

● *THE EYES*

Made up to look even more like saucers.

● *THE LIPS*

Painted with a hard gloss that makes them appear stuck together.

● *THE MASK*

Thick white make-up with the finish of a china plate.

All of this helped create the image of a frigid, aggressive, manipulating dragon. Perhaps much of this image sprang from the minds of males who felt threatened by such a strong woman. Now you will find out for yourself. The Joan we'll be doing today is the Real-Life Joan, unless you feel glamorous enough to tackle Early Tap-Dancing Joan, or weirded-out enough to go for Bad Late-Night Movie Joan (*Trog, Berserk,* etc.).

●●●●●●●●●●●●●●

PROPS REQUIRED

○ White make-up, thick bright lipstick
○ A three-foot-long stick
○ Blonde curly-haired girl doll
○ Container of Ajax
○ Wire clothes hanger
○ Hatchet
○ Bandana
○ Margaret Thatcher-style bomb-proof wig

●●●●●●●●●●●●●●

WHAT TO DO

① Place three-foot stick along shoulders inside jacket for Football Player-of-the-Year shoulder-pad look.
② Apply white mask of greasy make-up until you look like Marcel Marceau with sweating sickness.
③ Tie bandana over forehead.
④ Grab doll and shake it roughly. Scream and point to wire hanger.
⑤ With voice tailing upward, scream: "A $400 dress on a wire hanger?! No wire hangers!!! Ever!!!"
⑥ Thrash doll with hanger (taking care not to remove limbs, head, etc.).
⑦ Run into bathroom with doll. Fall on knees screaming.
⑧ Pull doll about roughly and fling Ajax all over the place.
⑨ Scream: "We'll scrub the floor together!!!"
⑩ Begin scrubbing with a cry of: "I'm not mad at you, I'm mad at the dirt!"

⑪ Jump up, grab hatchet. Cry: "Now let's go see the rose bushes!"

⑫ Stand up, take bow, doll too (what's left of it).

The main thing to remember with Joan is the action of the eyes. They stare directly at you, with the head tilted slightly back and the mouth pressed into a tight downward line. If they stared hard enough they could burn their way through ¼-inch plate steel.

For a simple everyday Joan Crawford, the kind you might suddenly need at the office, say, try this: Stuff small cushions into the shoulders of an old double-breasted jacket and button it up. Walk with the shoulders and the chin leading. Never smile. Turn your head suddenly and stare after people until you scorch their clothes. Sign things (napkins, 8 × 12 glossies, shirt fronts, etc.) Walk in a refined and ladylike manner, placing one foot directly in front of the other, but keep yourself drawn up to your full height while you do this, making your chest and shoulders as broad and square as a door. This can look very disconcerting on the right person. You should see our postman do it.

MAE WEST

●●●●●●●●●●●●●●●●

Look here, do we have to do this? Anyone can "do" Mae. Ask your mother to try after a couple of swigs of cooking sherry and she'll probably knock out as good a passing imitation of Ol' Piston Hips as anyone could.

There are really just a few things to remember.

① You are attempting to parody a parody. Mae's biggest imitator was herself.

② Mae never ever stood still. The hips were grinding away as if they were attached to a perpetual motion engine.

③ She rarely sat with her legs facing front. Better you sit with your body facing forward but with the legs together and to the side, with the arms raised to the back of the head.

④ Most important of all: Mae never looked at anyone, for any reason. Look at any photograph of Mae. Where are her eyes? Right, in the furthest corner of her face, studying the pigeons nesting in the rafters of the studio roof.

When she worked with W. C. Fields, their acting styles clashed so violently together that they probably never even made eye contact once during the entire shoot.

⑤ Mae was all curves. You may need to be padded with cushions. Then again, you may not, in which case my advice is trying

cottage cheese and an apple for lunch. *Voluptuous* was the word frequently applied to Mae's figure. Today we think of *voluptuous* as meaning *fat*.

⑥ You must learn to utter the expletive "Oh!" with a rollercoaster full of intonation, beginning from deep within the chest.

●●●●●●●●●●●●●●●●

WHAT TO DO

① Legs together, gyrate the hips and the bottom.

② Roll eyes to the rafters.

③ Place right hand on hip.

④ Gingerly touch back of hair with left hand.

⑤ Raise one eyebrow from time to time.

⑥ Never stop wobbling motion for an instant.

⑦ Repeat one of the following phrases:

CLASSIC MAE WEST CATCHPHRASES

"It's not the men in my life, but the life in my men."

"You better come up and see me." (She didn't say: "Come up and see me some time.")

"A hard man is good to find."

"Beulah, peel me a grape."

BRUCE LEE

●●●●●●●●●●●●●●●●●

How are the facial muscles doing? Beginning to seize up yet? Well, it's time for something different, something uniquely oriental. So oriental, in fact, that an hour after you've done this impression you'll feel like doing it again.

Bruce Lee, born Li Chen-Fan, ex–1958 Hong Kong Cha Cha King, never lived to see the peak of his popularity. At the time of his death, European audiences had seen few of his films. But now you can help keep the legend of Lee alive with your homage to the Master of the Flying Feet.

As with Fred and Ginger, you can avoid years of costly and time-consuming hospital treatment with a few simple precautions.

●●●●●●●●●●●●●●●●●

PROPS REQUIRED

○ One pair of baggy white pajamas
○ One bottle "Jungle Red" high gloss nail polish

●●●●●●●●●●●●●●●●●

PRECAUTIONS TO BE TAKEN PRIOR TO IMPRESSION

① Remove all sharp objects from room.
② Clear floor area of all low-lying surprise-bruise objects, i.e., trendy coffee tables.
③ Arrange pillows and cushions around edges of room to break fall of flying debris, i.e., friends standing too close when you show them your kick.
④ Tell neighbors to ignore blood-curdling screams, smashes, etc., for the next few minutes. Recommend name of a good plasterer in the event of being hurled against their dividing wall.

●●●●●●●●●●●●●●●●●

TIPS

You don't have to look Cantonese, but it helps. Masking tape over the eyelids is fine providing you do not attempt to remove it suddenly, or you may find yourself seeking the services of someone who knows how to put eyes back in.

Lee had a dangerous, insolent way of looking at his enemies, staring at them in a sidelong fashion. His movements were a contrasting combo of the superfast and the superslow.

Today we shall learn the Walk and the Kick. Breaking boards with the feet will be covered in another book entitled *Emotional Release Through DIY,* which will also feature a chapter called "Replacing Roofing Tiles with Your Forehead."

Acts such as kicking down brick walls with your bare toes, it must be remembered, were not performed by stars like Lee but by Chinese builders during housing crises.

●●●●●●●●●●●●●

THE BRUCE LEE WALK

① Place right foot sideways with toe pointing out to right.
② Place left foot so that toes point left, with heel of left foot touching toes of right foot.

③ Step one foot over the other with knee raised high.
④ Continue this walk throughout, raising knees high. You now look like a Chinese chicken.
⑤ With palms open, wheel arms over each other in "steam train" fashion.
⑥ Look around you at all times, moving slowly as if under water.
⑦ Keep elbows out, occasionally making a sudden move with one arm, as if lashing out at an unseen assailant.

⑧ Make wide shapes with your mouth, combined with sharp intakes of breath and exhalations reminiscent of someone standing on a piece of broken glass.

⑨ Suddenly drop low, bending the knees, bottom sticking out, body almost parallel to the floor.

⑩ Half close eyes suspiciously and slowly look sideways, accompanying this with a long, noisy intake of breath through a tiny O-shaped mouth.

⑪ With a high piercing scream, rush at surprised neighbor who dropped by to borrow a cup of rice and wrestle to the floor in an explosion of Uncle Ben's.

⑫ Stand up, face opponent and bow deeply.

● ● ● ● ● ● ● ● ● ● ● ● ● ●

THE BRUCE LEE KICK

At this point you may wish to try out your props.

Tear the top half of the pajamas so that your chest is exposed (how much you care to expose may be determined by your sex— or your lifestyle).

Paint four parallel lines of "Jungle Red" high gloss nail polish down one side of your chest, and also across the left cheek of your face. This gives you the "survivor of several surprise attacks" look, and can be seen sported by the Cha Cha King himself in *Enter the Dragon*.

O.K., we are now ready. Let's get out there and bust some Wedgwood.

① Using the walk, circle opponent warily, breathing in noisily through mouth.

② Remain facing opponent so that walk is performed sideways.

③ Slowly build up yell in throat, starting low and menacingly, growing higher and louder.

④ With yell at full throttle, leap into the air so that left leg flies straight out and right leg folds under buttocks. You should be about a foot from the ground.

⑤ At full stretch, left leg should be raised high so that foot is actually above head.

⑥ Don't actually hit anyone. The one impression you don't want to leave is that of the heel of your shoe on a friend's forehead.

⑦ Upon landing you must keep your balance. Uncoil slowly until upright. Push chest out and pull arms slowly back as if returning them to their proper place.

⑧ Let out long noisy breath through mouth.

It is worth remembering that Mr. Lee moved like an oiled, spring-loaded machine. Each movement was prefaced with a moment of the deepest concentration. Pausing to blow the nose or rearrange twisted underwear may well damage the illusion of Zen-like mysticism.

Steatopygic or other excessively developed persons may wish to sit this one out, and use the time to develop an impersonation of someone less physically demanding.

HUMPHREY BOGART

Apart from roles as gangsters or journalists uncovering scandals, Bogie will always be remembered as the lone private eye in movies like *The Maltese Falcon,* and has been so frequently impersonated that there was even a film made starring a Bogart look-alike entitled *The Man with Bogart's Face.*

Although his screen career did not begin until he was in his late thirties, Bogie created a series of unforgettable characterizations, roles which will be remembered years after your impression has been blotted from the memory. True, you could live on in people's minds by actually shooting someone in the finale, but this sort of behavior is generally frowned upon nowadays.

To carry off a passable Bogart successfully, you must learn some forties vocabulary. You can pick this up by simply rereading old Raymond Chandler and Dashiell Hammett novels.

PROPS REQUIRED

○ A beige trenchcoat
○ A brown slouch hat
○ A pack of cigarettes

WORDS YOU WILL REQUIRE

Try teaming up these words to form phrases. For example:

Sweetheart

Double-Cross

Bimbo

Hardware (gun, not store)

Lousy

Broad

Dime Store

Two-Timing

Bum

Punk

Frame-Up

Flatfoot

Stoolie

Two-Bit

Stacked

Big Cheese

Goons

Squealer

Dame

and so on.

Two-bit double-crossing punk

BOGIE AS SPADE OR MARLOWE

① Turn collar of raincoat half up.

② Pull hat down over eyes.

③ Thrust hands deep into pockets.

④ Come in through door by opening it with your shoulder.

⑤ Remove one hand from pocket and push up hat to the back of the head.

⑥ Keeping head down, flick eyes up at person opposite. Withdraw pack of cigarettes and light one with head still down.

⑦ Flick up eyes, draw in smoke, and keep cigarette pointing vertically down to floor at all times.

⑧ Look as sullen and tired as possible. Say: "O.K., sweetheart, how about you and me havin' a little talk?"

⑨ Pronounce "Sweetheart" with a lisp. "Schweetheart."

⑩ At end of sentence give a quick mirthless grin using the mouth only. The eyes must remain cold. The grin should last for about a quarter of a second. This is performed repeatedly, like a nervous tic.

⑪ When speaking, it is important to move the mouth as little as possible (except for the nervous tic-grin) and to speak from the back of the throat. A good practice sentence is the following Bogie phrase: "I never met a dame that ditten unnerstand a schmack in the mouth." (This phrase is not recommended for use in public, especially at feminist rallies.)

HOW TO SEARCH A HOTEL ROOM FOR HIRED KILLERS, BOGIE STYLE

This "search-the-place-for-hired-goons-lying-in-wait" method was also a favorite of Alan Ladd's, and can easily be carried out in your living room.

① Stand outside door, listening.

② Check hair placed across door with thumb. It is broken.

③ Raise gun by bending elbow until gun is pointing upright near face. (How they managed to avoid blowing their ears off I'll never know.)

④ Turn body at right angles to door and suddenly open it wide with free arm.

⑤ Enter room by sliding around door with your back, gun arm still raised.

⑥ Turn head to far left and walk sideways right.

⑦ Cross room to drapes. Suddenly beat them and rip them back.

⑧ Continue crablike walk to bathroom door (this being a hotel room, the bathroom adjoins it) still with head turned in opposite direction so that you cannot see where you are walking. I don't know why private eyes do this, but they do.

⑨ Vanish suddenly into bathroom. Suddenly whip back out again.

⑩ Spot open window. Run to it and look out up fire escape. Mutter: "Damn!"

ALTERNATIVE BOGIE POSES

● A. THE DETECTIVE WITHOUT A CASE

① Remove jacket. Keep hat on back of head.

② Attach cycle clips to forearms of shirt.
③ Lean back in swivel chair.
④ Put feet up on desk, cross legs at ankles.
⑤ Fold arms behind head.
⑥ Blow smoke rings.
⑦ Wait for shadow of mystery woman to appear on office door.

⬤ *B. THE CASABLANK STARE*

① Don white jacket and bow tie.
② Sit hunched at table, hands touching, forearms flat, elbows pointing out.
③ Look disconsolately at bottle of whisky before you.

④ Pick it up, empty last drop into glass.
⑤ Toss it back in one swift movement of arm.
⑥ Resist temptation to say the incorrect line: "Play it again, Sam."

If your impersonation is not perfect, don't worry. Private eyes were really not very bright. I mean, if you thought that there was a killer standing fully dressed in your bath with a gun trained on you, would you honestly rip open the shower curtain? Forget it, call Room Service.

GERARD DEPARDIEU

One of the most interesting and important new actors to emerge from France in years, Gerard Depardieu is Europe's answer to Richard Gere—an updated Brando with the new male sensibilities of the eighties.

Although he has already clocked up an impressive number of excellent and often avant-garde films, his name is only just becoming familiar to non-Francophiles.

The Gerard Depardieu we are doing today will be the subtitled version. If you prefer your impersonation in the dubbed version, you must be prepared to have a friend hide behind you shouting your lines in a ridiculous Bronx accent. The modulation of your friend's speech should have absolutely no bearing whatsoever on what is actually being said. It is important that the opening and closing of your mouth should in no way be related to the dialogue being heard, either.

PROPS REQUIRED

- Ten white T-shirts
- Jeans
- Toothpick
- Flick knife
- Strips of paper
- Pen
- Sweat

WHAT TO DO

① Put on all ten T-shirts at once. I am assuming you do not have the gigantic muscular build of Depardieu. (Ideally, you should have a physique that's a cross between the Incredible Hulk and Joan Crawford.)

② Chew a toothpick insolently. Trudge about with your hands in your pockets.

③ Lower your eyebrows and stare out moodily from under them. Slump against a wall. Clean your nails with the flick knife. Press your lips hard together.

④ Have someone bump into you and give them a look as if you are about to rip their head off.

⑤ Rip open a beer can and slug the contents down in one. Wipe your mouth with the back of your hand.

⑥ Your ten T-shirts should ensure that you are sweating up a storm. Good.

⑦ A girl passes. Stare at her so hard that you burn right through her clothes and leave scorchmarks on the opposite wall.

⑧ Wipe your forehead and, keeping your mouth small and tight, say quietly: "*Voulez-vous venir chez moi pour un petit peu de...*" Raise one eyebrow and lick your lips slowly.

⑨ Now hold up a strip of paper at waist level, reading: "Hi!"

⑩ Lean forward and run your hand across your chest slowly. Say: "*Mon hôtel n'est qu'à deux kilomètres d'ici.*"

⑪ Hold up another piece of paper reading: "Gee, you're cute!"

You may continue in this fashion for as long as you like. Just make sure that what you say has nothing to do with what they read. Now you know why subtitled movies are so confusing.

Feel free to resolve the story in a manner which includes:

○ **A.** Cruelly crushing a woman's lips against yours.

○ **B.** Having a knife fight in the street.

Note: It would be best if you avoided reenacting Depardieu's final scene in Ferreri's *The Last Woman,* in which Gerard reduced cinema hot dog sales in one swoop when he cut off his willy with a carving knife.

BETTE MIDLER

●●●●●●●●●●●●●●

Now here's a nice noisy impersonation for the more raucously inclined among you. The divine Miss M, ex-bath house chanteuse and current concert superstar, provides us with an excellent impression suitable for livening up any gathering, from a Christian Scientist Reading Circle to a postnatal exercise class.

Here we have proof that Loud can be Funny if combined with Talent. We are, of course, expecting you to prove the latter.

Many impersonations can be performed without props, but here a little dress sense will help you create the role much more easily.

Actually, you could do this whole impersonation with the aid of just a two-foot-long piece of parcel string.

●●●●●●●●●●●●●●

THE OUTFIT

○ Very high heels (ideally red patent leather)
○ A dress three sizes too small (ideal fabric: fake leopardskin with plastic belt)
○ Gingery wig (try backcombing and applying hair spray to a mop-head)

Bette Midler's distinctive style owes much to an exclusive movement she has taken years to perfect: the Stagger. You can create this movement after a simple painful

lesson in body torture. First, cut the top off of the dress, as low as you dare and then some. Alternatively, wear one so tight that you'd need major surgery to inhale.

Slip into the high heels. If they do not force your legs forward into a standing version of a runner's starting position, then you are not high up enough. Add blocks of paper inside the backs of the shoes.

Take the wig and leave it on the front porch for at least twenty-four hours. After this time has elapsed, bring it in and put it straight on your head. Do not comb it. You may add a seashell or an ashtray to your coiffure in order to enhance whatever it is that it already has at the moment.

Having done this, turn to your mirror reflection. Notice that the stance of your body resembles the letter W on its side.

If you prefer not to bother with the outfit, you may prepare for the Midler Stagger by tying the aforementioned piece of parcel string just above the joints of your knees. This will have the same constricting effect as the dress, and should have an unusual effect on your walking ability. Practice away from sharp, protruding objects.

●●●●●●●●●●●●●●

THE MIDLER STAGGER

① Chest out.
② Bottom out.
③ Thighs welded together (all motion

from below the knees only).

④ Arms away from the body with elbows up and level to ribcage.

⑤ Wrists loose and broken-looking.

⑥ Launch yourself across the room taking fast tiny steps, and swing the arms back and forth from above the elbow as you go.

At this point it would be a good idea to have a microphone handy. This Honolulu Baby makes good use of it, clutching it high to the chest, screaming, and running all at the same time.

●●●●●●●●●●●●●●●●●●

FACIAL EXPRESSIONS

There are only two of these you need worry about:

① *THE SMILE*

When Bette smiles, you really know you've been beamed at. The whole face lights up as the lips, tight and closed, form a crescent moon, and the eyes echo this shape in inverted sealed crescents.

② *THE SCREAM*

This comes during the top notes in a number, or during the fastest part of a song, as in the end of "Friends." Accompanying the scream is a look perfected by Joe Cocker—that of a scrunched-up ball of agonized facial features atop a mass of straining neck veins. The voice must be slightly hoarse, tailing up at the end of a sentence instead of down, and *loud*. It must be packed with intonation and clar-it-y, so that each utterance contains about, oh, say, three or four dramatic sentences' worth of tonal effects.

The Bette Midler act is pretty much the same act Mae West would have done if she had been born much later and had just had six cups of coffee and a handful

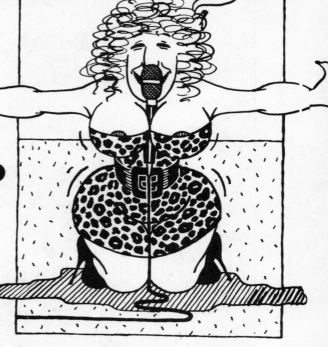

of really speedy diet pills, you know, the little blue ones that make you talk so fast nobody can understand a word you're saying.

●●●●●●●●●●●●●●●

THINGS YOU MUST BE PREPARED TO DO AS BETTE MIDLER

① Drop on to your knees with microphone clutched between breasts.

② Lay on back with legs waggling wide apart in the air.

③ Do a handstand.

④ Lay on your stomach across a stool.

⑤ Expose your breasts if someone asks to see them.

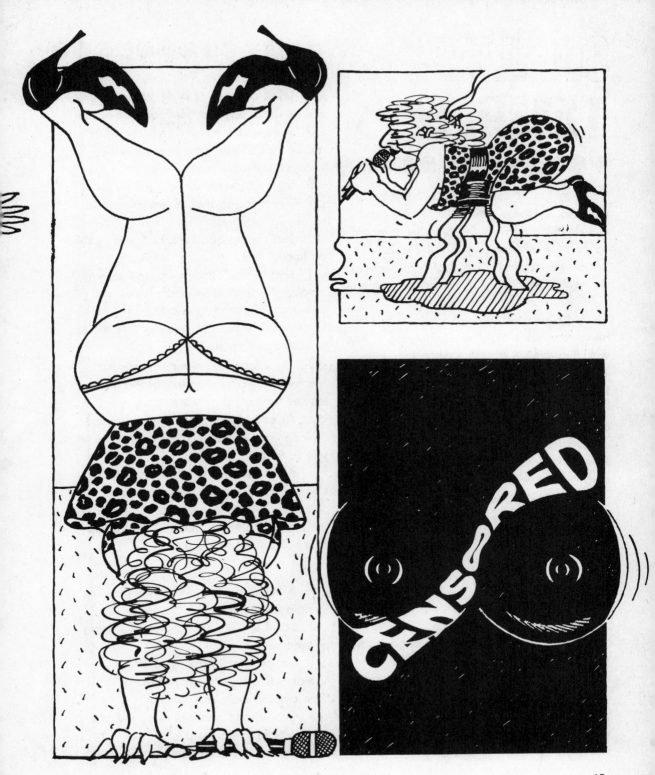

SHIRLEY TEMPLE

●●●●●●●●●●●●●●●●

Ugh, child stars. The only consolation we have concerning these terminally cute and repulsive mites is the fact that they grow up to be weird-looking baby-faced has-beens who attempt their final comebacks at the age of twenty-three advertising toilet rolls.

Not so with Shirley Temple, who still makes the news. Still, there's nothing wrong with Tatum O'Neal that a really hard slap wouldn't have sorted out, says your mother. But what does she know?

Shirley Temple was the most popular child star ever, and in just four years sang and danced her way through over twenty movies. In order to carry off your performance as the tousled moppet successfully, you may feel it necessary to don a gingham party dress with petticoats, ankle socks, and sandals.

That's up to you, of course. I have no say in your private life.

This impression works best to music. See if you can find a copy of the following: "Animal Crackers in My Soup," "On the Good Ship Lollipop," "I Wanna Be Loved by You," "Tomorrow."

Of course, this last record is modern, but sounds as if it were written with Baby Shirley in mind. Don't you *hate* it? Actually, any cracked old forties record will do if you play it at the wrong speed.

●●●●●●●●●●●●●●●●

WHAT TO DO

① Look perky, eyes wide, roaming back and forth for appreciation from the adults.
② Peep out from under curls. Blow unruly lock of hair from eyes in mock-annoyed fashion.
③ Stamp foot petulantly.
④ Tug front of dress down from time to time.
⑤ Puff cheeks out, rock back and forth on heels.
⑥ For chorus, march up and down holding the sides of your dress out and swinging your arms to and fro.
⑦ Poke tongue out cheekily, just the tip, eyes screwed up tight.
⑧ Try a little tap, swinging arms back and forth together, top half of the body leaning forward as you stamp away.
⑨ At end, stamp foot, bend knee, and flourish arms wide. This lets them know that you've finished.
⑩ A cute smile and a little curtsy. Giggle. Look pleased with yourself and adorable and sweet. Applaud audience back, holding hands out. Continue this until you actually hear someone being sick.

A friend has her own version of Shirley Temple to perform:
① Stand up very straight. Look terribly pleased with self.
② Recite the following in sing-song fashion while tugging hem of dress: "I'm a little teapot, short and stout…"
③ Crook right arm and place right hand on hip. "Here's my handle…"
④ Instead of holding other arm out

straight like spout, crook it, placing left hand on hip. "Here's my other handle..."

⑤ Look down in puzzlement at one arm, then the other. "Shit, I'm a sugarbowl."

⑥ Stamp foot, blow, etc., etc.

A THOUGHT

Bearing in mind that Shirley Temple grew up to enter the political arena as an ambassador, the thought of a country governed in the not-too-distant future by Brooke Shields is enough to make you want to go and draw all your money out of the bank.

MARLON
BRANDO

●●●●●●●●●●●●●●●

Our Marlon is available in two distinctive modes: Early and Late. The former is filled with inarticulate rage and sullen brooding sexuality. The latter is filled with inarticulate rage and sullen, er...you will need two sets of props and an enormous ego (something you may not possess in any quantity after tackling some of the previous impersonations).

But don't let the booing of your audience depress you. Give 'em something from *A Streetcar Named Desire* when they least expect it.

Let's begin with Early Surly Brando... the menace, the untamed sex, the insolent mumble. The problem is, how to achieve that elusive "Brando" state of mind?

●●●●●●●●●●●●●●●

DEVELOPING BRANDO'S CHARISMA

① GET ANGRY

Turn up the thermostat and raise the temperature of the place by ten degrees. Sweat. Have someone insult you. Get a pretty girl to snub you and walk away laughing. Have someone tip a drink over you. Read a government pamphlet. Open an envelope from the *Reader's Digest* telling you that you may already have won a fortune. Try to get the thermosealed plastic off a new record album without using your teeth. You should now be angry.

② BE A REBEL

Break from conformity. Fold a Neil Diamond album in half. Watch documentaries for college students about diseased rats. Ask to see the wine list in Burger King. Paint the inside of your mouth lilac. Travel across town via the sewer system. Take your banker to dinner in a bowling alley. Visit an oil spill just to watch the seagulls having a hard time. You are now a rebel.

③ BECOME INARTICULATE

Drink a quart of Chivas Regal with Malibu and Dr. Pepper chasers. Bounce a grapefruit off what used to be the "soft" part of your skull until it becomes soft again. Damage your IQ by listening to Andrew Lloyd Webber albums. Breathe bleach fumes for two hours, then go and sit in the sun. You are now inarticulate.

Now let's get started before this all wears off.

●●●●●●●●●●●●●●●

EARLY BRANDO: PROPS REQUIRED

○ Tight-leg denims
○ Hair grease
○ T-shirt with an inverted triangular sweat stain down the front

●●●●●●●●●●●●●●●

WHAT TO DO

① Slick hair back, lean with one arm

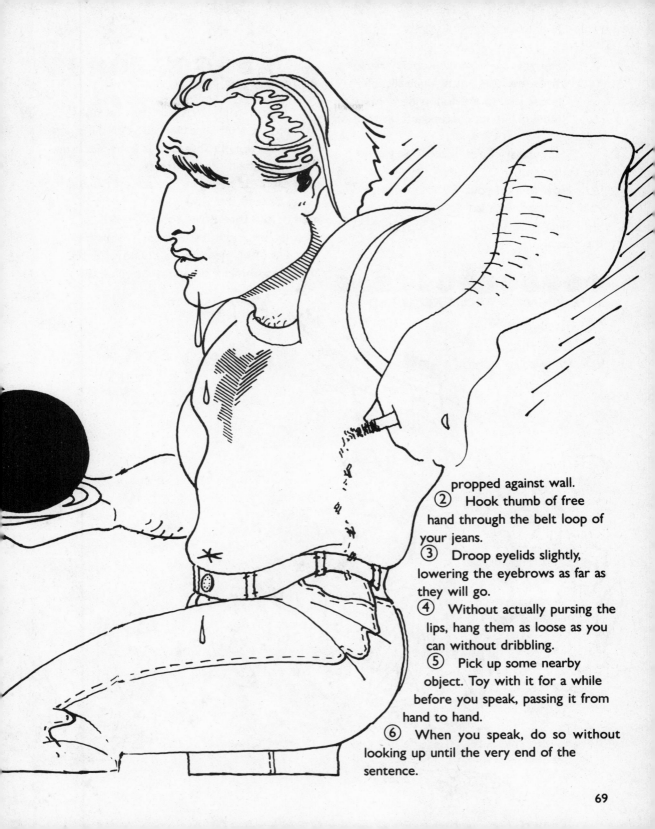

propped against wall.

② Hook thumb of free hand through the belt loop of your jeans.

③ Droop eyelids slightly, lowering the eyebrows as far as they will go.

④ Without actually pursing the lips, hang them as loose as you can without dribbling.

⑤ Pick up some nearby object. Toy with it for a while before you speak, passing it from hand to hand.

⑥ When you speak, do so without looking up until the very end of the sentence.

⑦ Keep your jaws and lips totally slack. Your words must be almost unintelligible.

⑧ Choose one of the following phrases:

"I coulda been a contender...instead of a bum."

"Hey, canary bird! Toots! Get out of the bathroom!"

⑨ Now pull off your T-shirt and wipe your forehead with it.

⑩ Sling it on the floor and lope out of the room.

●●●●●●●●●●●●●●●●●●

LATE BRANDO: PROPS REQUIRED

○ Tuxedo
○ Cottonballs
○ Wing-collar shirt

●●●●●●●●●●●●●●●●●●

WHAT TO DO

If your sylph-like figure fails to flesh out the tuxedo, stuff a cushion up your shirt. Purely for the purpose of this impersonation, you understand. Remove it before your next black-tie function. We are, of course, doing Brando the Godfather, his most memorable Late Role. You may wish to attempt Brando in *Last Tango in Paris*, for which you will need half a pound of butter and a broad mind, or *Apocalypse Now*, for

which you have to shave your head and sit in the dark muttering: "The horror...the horror" for hours.

Let's stick to Don Corleone. To a heavyweight body we add a full face, by simply filling your cheeks with the cottonballs until your jowls hang down like an aged bloodhound. This is known as the "Robert Morley Effect."

Now hood your eyes. Mumble. Snap your fingers and make a fast "come hither" motion with your hand at your side to indicate to the henchman standing behind you that he should rush forward and pin the person you are addressing to the floor by sitting on his arms. Look at people by turning your whole body toward them. Raise your head to see their faces, rather than your eyelids. Finally, stagger out into the garden and die in the flowerbed to the strains of mandolin music. A friend of mine

surmounted the problem of having cottonballs in his mouth for the duration of a fancy-dress party by filling them with gin.

Unfortunately he got drunk, swallowed several of them and spent the rest of the evening sitting in the corner coughing like a cat trying to bring up hairballs. Remember that even though you are the Godfather, suggesting to someone that the two of you "go to the mattresses" can still get you a smack in the jowls. All in all, Early Brando is more fun than Late Brando, because, just like Orson Welles, we had all the good stuff first, with the later years spent remaining virtually immobile with the exception of moving the writing hand for the signing of large checks.

MARILYN MONROE

Just remember Marilyn's own words: "I'm not interested in the money. I just want to be wonderful." Assuming that nobody will be willing to pay you for your impression, you'll have to settle for just being wonderful too. You will have to cultivate the wide-eyed innocent stare, the vocal and physical wiggle, the tragic aura of the torch singer.

But the best way to become wonderful is to feel wonderful first, so it's off to the liquor cabinet for a toothmug-full of something that's been matured for about twelve years. Now, before unsteadiness sets in, let's go to it.

PROPS REQUIRED

- A long scarf
- A vacuum cleaner
- White low-cut dress (optional)

WHAT TO DO

① Seconds before attempting impersonation, apply high gloss lipstick. (The amount required varies from person to person, but gloss should be bright enough to heliograph a message no less than half a mile under cloudy conditions.)

② Drape scarf over neck and behind shoulders so that ends hang down back.

③ Become highly conscious of your body as you walk. Legs together, rear moving from side to side as you shift weight from the top of one leg to the other.

④ As you put weight on to left leg, dip left shoulder.

⑤ Do the same with right leg and dip right shoulder. Repeat. Imagine you are walking next to Jane Russell in *Gentlemen Prefer Blondes*. Imagine that everyone is staring at your body.

⑥ Stop. Keep thighs together and place hands on them. Lean forward suggestively.

⑦ Hunch up shoulders. Arms in, squeezing breasts upward and together.

⑧ Close eyes. Stretch neck forward. Purse lips and blow kiss with small "Pooh" noise.

⑨ Let out small squeal and giggle.

Hoover

BEST MONROE MUSIC

"I Wanna Be Loved by You"
"Runnin' Wild"
"Two Little Girls from Little Rock"
(you will need a friend for this)
"That Old Black Magic"

"Diamonds Are
a Girl's Best Friend"
"Heat Wave"
"After You Get What You Want You Don't Want It"

Remember, everything about Marilyn wiggles, especially the singing voice—a high-pitched breathiness you should attempt now before the drink you so ungraciously slugged back really begins to get a grip on your liver.

● **THE** SOME LIKE IT HOT *STANCE*
(Small banjo optional)

① Keeping banjo in pit of stomach, strum while sliding right leg up left knee.

② Smile with your teeth together and wink right eye.

③ High kick twice, continue strumming banjo.

④ Throw head back, laugh with mouth wide open.

● THE "HEAT WAVE" BUMP

① Using music to help you,

73

throw arms in air, touch hands together and hold them at the back of the head.

② Move elbows inward forcing hair over eyes.

③ Assume W position (see "Bette Midler").

④ Move area below waist (i.e., bottom and other sundry parts) in and out.

⑤ Keeping thighs together, wiggle rear from side to side.

● THE RIVER OF NO RETURN GRIND

① Split dress up sides. Stand with legs apart so that thighs poke out of dress.

② Hold arms straight out wide on either side of you.

③ Move the top half of your body from side to side without moving your legs.

④ Quickly wiggle your shoulders back and forth as you go. (This will shimmy the breasts. You may wish to anchor them with guy ropes, tarpaulins, etc.)

There are many other actions you can perform as Marilyn, but the best bets are ones involving the eyes (wide, innocent, or closed completely) and the lips (pursed together in a kiss or wide and showing zillions of teeth).

Remember that a kiss is a dangerous weapon in Marilyn's hands, so before you blow one be careful where you point it.

Now, about the vacuum cleaner. You will need an attachment.

● MARILYN AND VACUUM CLEANER

① Place vacuum cleaner with attached nozzle on floor with pipe pointing upward.

② Turn cleaner to blow.

③ Stand over nozzle with legs wide apart.

④ Lean forward, place hands together flat on tops of knees.

⑤ Look up, give wide smile and laugh.

⑥ Dress should be blowing up at sides. If you are being sprayed with dirt, have vacuum cleaner repaired.

⑦ Remember to wear underwear.

JANET ANTHONY LEIGH & PERKINS: *A PSYCHO MINIDRAMA*

●●●●●●●●●●●●●●●●

In our search for simple, powerful impersonations that even an elderly relative could recognize from a distance, we must inevitably take a trip to the bathroom. For here the stage is already set for a stirring little vignette which will live on in the hearts and lower intestines of all who witness it.

You will need a large damp cloth to mop up with.

●●●●●●●●●●●●●●●●

PROPS REQUIRED

○ Bath with a shower curtain
○ Kitchen knife
○ Old black dress
○ Gray wig
○ Bathrobe
○ Leotard
○ Bottle of ketchup (or water soluble red paint)
○ Bulb-ended chicken baster
○ A copy of Bernard Herrman's score for *Psycho* (optional)

You will need a friend. (After this you'll need all the friends you can get.)

●●●●●●●●●●●●●●●●

PREPARATION

The person impersonating Janet Leigh dons the leotard. In *Psycho* we never see her entirely naked and there is no reason to start now. Over this the bathrobe is worn. The person playing Norman Bates, owner of the world's most infamous motel, should be responsible for filling the chicken baster with ketchup and tying it to the kitchen knife. He then dons dress and wig.

●●●●●●●●●●●●●●●●

PERFORMANCE DIRECTIONS

① *Janet* reaches over the bathtub and turns on the shower.

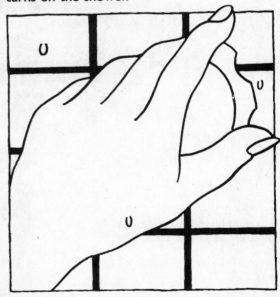

② *Janet* stands upright and lets the robe fall around her feet.
③ *Janet* steps daintily into the shower.
④ *Janet* raises her hands beneath her

chin, palms facing, as she enjoys cascading water.

⑤ *Janet* caresses her neck as water hits her face.

⑥ *Tony* approaches shower curtain with knife held face-high in the right hand.

⑦ *Janet* turns to see shadow of *Tony* on shower curtain.

⑧ *Tony* rips shower curtain back suddenly. (It helps if you get Track One, Side Two of the *Psycho* album to coincide with this action.)

⑨ *Janet* screams and screams, holding her hands up at her chest and neck, falling against the back wall of the shower. *Tony* makes (fake) stabs with knife.

⑩ *Tony* squeezes the bulb of the chicken baster and squirts ketchup everywhere as he stabs.

⑪ *Janet* screams and turns her back to the killer as *Tony* continues stabbing motions in smooth forty-five-degree arcs, moving the forearm only.

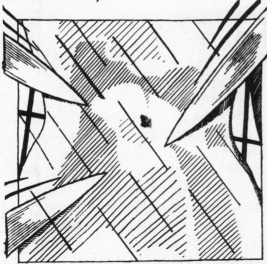

⑫ *Janet* slowly slides down shower wall with her nails scraping tiles.

⑬ *Janet* turns around to continue sliding down wall and outstretches her right arm in front of her.

⑭ *Janet* clutches shower curtain and pulls it down as she topples over.

⑮ *Janet* lands hanging half out of the bath with her left cheek pressed against the floor tiles, staring straight ahead. Chin and nose should be touching the tiles.

Note: Plastic knives with retractable blades never look authentic. Care should be used with a real kitchen knife during the stabbing sequence, and the ketchup should obscure the fact that the blade is not actually entering flesh. If it is entering the flesh you are doing this impersonation *wrong* and such an action could result in your not being invited to the host's house again. I must go, mother's calling.

JOAN RIVERS

●●●●●●●●●●●●●●

This mistress of the Great American One-Liner is the talk of social gatherings (Tupperware parties, garage sales) everywhere.

Physical similarities are a help here, so if you are built like a stick, own a mouth that was once used as a blueprint for the entrance to the Holland Tunnel, and have a head which looks like it spent six years in a cider press, you're in luck.

It's a fact (read the *National Enquirer* if you really want to know) that no one has ever seen Joan Rivers with her mouth shut. Maybe it doesn't close at all. It's probably jammed.

Here is the original Motor Mouth, and the engine is definitely revving too high. Joan, in her effort to put a gag across at the speed of sound, often breaks that barrier and passes her own words on the way back. Sometimes the second half of her sentence arrives before she has finished with the first half and comes out of her mouth at the same time. The effect is like hearing a regular sentence fall down a flight of stairs.

Frequently, the second half of the sentence never arrives, because the next joke has come in early. Instead, the words halt for a sharp breath, and a catchphrase drops in. Often the set-up to the punchline is repeated with emphasis, while the slammer is delivered at great speed, almost thrown away, with a cry of "Oh yes!" stamped on the end.

The biggest problem in impersonating Joan Rivers is gearing up to her speed of delivery. The best way to achieve this is by taking cheap drugs (sniffing baking powder, inhaling drain stripper, etc.) to the point where the lyrics of records played at 78 rpm sound like normal speech to you.

The best way to tackle Joan is to sit on a tall stool, hands on thighs, leaning forward. Joan leads with the mouth, lipstick thin and mouth wedged permanently open in an upright oval.

●●●●●●●●●●●●●●

WHAT TO DO

① Hold your hands out in front of you, fingers spread, palms down.

② Say hoarsely: "Can we talk here?"

③ As you speak, make little patting movements with your hands to emphasize your words.

④ Tell a joke: "I'm not saying Liz Taylor is fat…" (Say very quickly again) "I'mnotsayingshe'sfat…but she's the only woman I know who can give an 'I speak your weight' machine laryngitis."

⑤ If people groan, lean forward, give the room a one-eighty, slap your hands on your thighs and say: "Oh come on!"

⑥ Sit back upright, put your hands on your hips and say: "Oh, grow up!"

The good Joan Rivers impersonator cultivates a Bronx accent and takes frequent noisy deep breaths through the mouth. Other Rivers trademarks include a regular cry of: "Oh, look how quiet the room got!"

INSTANT IMPERSONATIONS

●●●●●●●●●●●●●●●●

There will be times when your new fame as an impressionist catches up with you, and will demand that you enact a character for the edification of others at short notice. It is at this time that the following *instant impersonations* can be trotted out and dismissed.

●●●●●●●●●●●●●●●●

1. BOY GEORGE

Has Dad got some plain old pajamas? Has Auntie got a baggy white hat and heavy pale blue eye shadow? Good. Now shave your eyebrows to points and wash your hair in Gravy Mix. Mime to the song "Time (Clock of the Heart)."

DO NOT mime to "Do You Really Want to Hurt Me." Somebody might.

●●●●●●●●●●●●●●●●

2. LIZ TAYLOR

Wear stage jewelry. Eat. Wear a too low-cut, too tight outfit. Keep eating. Giggle like a little girl trapped in a big body. Keep your hand in front of your mouth when you do so. Your voice must be as light and soft as a marshmallow. Put little breathy catches in your sentences. Keep giggling until people think there's something wrong with you. (There is.)

●●●●●●●●●●●●●●●●

3. CAROL CHANNING

Apply your lipstick in the dark. Apply your eye make-up with a spaghetti fork. Bat your eyelids, roll your eyes. Your lashes should look like creosoted garden rake prongs. Now talk like a duck. Wear tons of fake diamonds. Take beauty tips from Barbara Cartland.

●●●●●●●●●●●●●●●●

4. MARTY FELDMAN

Comb your hair with a toilet brush.

Cut up an egg box and place two of the compartments over your eyes. Draw pupils on the far sides of the compartments.

5. VIVIEN LEIGH

Flounce. Develop a Southern accent. Lower your face, raising your eyes imploringly until you get your own way. Twirl. Show off the dress. Give everyone in the room a peck on the cheek. Look fragile and spoiled. Faint dead away.

6. JULIE ANDREWS

A fifties dress from mother, preferably a schoolteachery one with a bib at the front. Skip. Train a parakeet to sit on your finger while you sing to it. Hit high, warbling notes with a smile on your face. See if butter will melt in your mouth. Try to change your image and fail.

7. DIANA ROSS

See Michael Jackson.

8. MICHAEL JACKSON

See Diana Ross.

9. LIBERACE

Sit at the piano. Place candlesticks on it. Smile. Sparkle. Simper. Turn collar up on jacket. Sprinkle clothes with sequins. If anybody looks at part of what you're wearing, hold it closer for them to see and tell them how much it cost. Favorite suit: spangled. Least favorite suit: palimony.

10. BENNY HILL

Pull an old trilby down over your ears, bending them in half. Put on old wire-framed glasses. Smile lasciviously. Grab the bottom of the first woman in a short dress that passes. Set sexual equality back about, oh, fifteen years or so.

11. JANE RUSSELL

Find a hayloft and sit in it. Place left hand on hip. Place right hand and elbow high on hay bale. Place legs to right side. Wear a low-cut T-shirt slipped below left shoulder. Hide bulky kitchen utensils (cuisinart, wok, steak hammer) down front of shirt. Pout.

12. DEAN MARTIN

Just stay in the kitchen with the drinks.

Italian barbers your father used to go to. Prowl. Bare your teeth. Narrow your eyes. Strike poses. Appear profile and full on, but never at a forty-five-degree angle. Wear the jacket part of a mohair suit with no shirt on underneath. Take a whip to a disco. Place hands on either end of whip handle and bite center of handle. Stay like this until someone takes a photograph.

15. PIA ZADORA

By the time this book comes out, will anyone remember her?

Fill your cheeks with cottonballs left over from Marlon Brando. Wear a minuscule spangly dress. Squeal, wiggle, and run. Peer out from under your fringe. Bounce. Pout. Remove eye make-up so that pupils appear the size of pinholes. Have Orson Welles praise you (the easiest part).

13. ESTHER WILLIAMS

Wear a white one-piece bathing suit and matching cap. Stick a flower on the side of the cap. Find a pool and swim in an arc with your arms by your sides and your eyes wide open. Your mouth should be in a fixed smile, with your teeth interlocked so that water cannot enter. Sink slowly into pool with a sparkler burning in each hand.

14. GRACE JONES

Have your hair cut at the half-blind

IF ALL ELSE FAILS

Be Yourself
(God Forbid!)

IMPERSONATIONS THAT REQUIRE
NO EFFORT OR TALENT AT ALL

While the rest of us are rolling our eyes, dragging our facial muscles beyond their limits of elasticity and flinging our limbs about like deranged aerobics instructors, there may be those who prefer to sit quietly in a corner, snuggled deep into a bean bag with a large gin, watching the rest of us make complete idiots of ourselves.

For those people who are either:

A. Too lazy to get involved;

B. Residing on a too chemically elevated cosmic plane to cope with what's going on...
...this page is dedicated.

WHAT TO DO

Everyone is doing impersonations. Someone comes over and asks you who *you* are going to impersonate. Lie there still for a second and then inform them that you have just finished your impression of a famous person. When they ask who, tell them one of the following:

① *RICHARD DREYFUSS*
Playing the car-crash victim paralyzed from the neck down in *Whose Life Is It Anyway?*

② *SIR WINSTON CHURCHILL*
Asleep during all-night war debate.

③ *R2D2*
Waiting for a new battery pack to be delivered.

④ *EARL WILLIAMS*
The convict in the Hecht and MacArthur play *The Front Page.* Spends virtually entire performance inside roll-top desk.

⑤ *PRINCE "CATERPILLAR MAN" RANDIAN*
A human torso who used to roll cigarettes with his lips.

⑥ *ORSON WELLES BETWEEN COMMERCIALS*
Impression is helped by balancing a large tray of party snacks on chest.

⑦ *CHARLOTTE BRONTË*
Dead.

⑧ *LASSIE*
Taking well-earned nap after rescuing little girl from collapsing mine shaft.

⑨ *ADOLF HITLER*
I'm not? Prove it.

⑩ *WALT DISNEY*
Gently defrosting in cryogenic freezer.

⑪ *JIMMY HOFFA*
Make like a block of cement.

⑫ *BO DEREK*
Demonstrating acting technique.

ALL-PURPOSE GENERIC
IMPERSONATION

●●●●●●●●●●●●●●●

Famous people do not act in public like ordinary people. They are above the common herd, and naturally expect to command more attention than regular human beings. Impersonating a famous person, therefore, brings many advantages. Faster service in restaurants. Courtesy from public officials. Window seats on trains and in airplanes. Second helpings of chocolate pudding. And now you too can have these things.

Your bearing and manner must create the feeling among onlookers that you are an extremely wealthy and famous person traveling incognito.

You must make them rack their brains trying to remember which TV show they have seen you on.

The aura you must create is a subtle one, for, having drawn attention to yourself, you must then disown it. You must appear *riche* but not *nouveau,* conspicuous, but not aware that you are so.

This does not mean you should go around looking like Jimmy Saville or Willie Nelson. Quite the reverse.

●●●●●●●●●●●●●●●

WHAT TO WEAR

Your clothes should look expensive and totally inappropriate to your surroundings.

Try wearing full evening dress in a greasy spoon. A Giorgio Armani jacket never fails to draw attention in a welfare line. A Dior gown has the same effect when worn in a bus station.

Note: When visiting these places dressed as above, make sure you know where your credit cards are and check on them regularly. Your conduct in these places should match your dress. For example, if a bum offers you a drink in a bus station, wipe the top of the bottle on your gown before drinking from it.

●●●●●●●●●●●●●●●

HOW TO ACT

① Have a friend run up to you in the street and take a photograph with a flash camera.

② Have someone come up to you in a bar and ask for your autograph. Act annoyed that your cover has been blown, but discreetly oblige.

③ Be paged when arriving at an airport.

④ When seated alone in a bar or restaurant, look at your watch by straightening your arm, swinging it above your head and lowering your wrist in front of your face. People will think you are a dancer.

⑤ If you wish to foster the "famous dancer" image, try this when standing at the bar with a drink. Lift up your left leg and lay it straight along the top of the bar. Lower

your head on to your foot as if modelling for Degas. (If you are male, do not try this in a rough neighborhood.)

⑥ If you are a woman, never appear with less than three dinner-jacketed male friends around you. Withdraw a cigarette and have them all rush to light it for you. If possible, always make your entrance from the top of a staircase.

⑦ Have your friends hustle you at great speed through a hotel lobby. Keep your head down and walk fast. Wear shades, but try not to trip over anything. Nothing damages one's air of worldly sophistication more than sprawling flat on one's face in public.

⑧ If involved in an altercation in a restaurant, never say: "Do you know who I am?" Only nobodies say that. Instead, say in a gently menacing voice: "Before pressing your point, I'd like you to think about your career here for a moment."

⑨ When seated in a restaurant, have someone else order for you. Get them to wipe your cutlery clean. Make them taste your food for you to see if it is too hot. At the end of the meal, wave the bill away.

⑩ Arrange for a genuinely famous person to greet you loudly in a restaurant. When they do, completely ignore them.

⑪ Always have a secretary running behind you taking notes.

⑫ Sit only in the backs of vehicles. Obviously one must choose one's mode of transportation with great care. Even wearing a ballgown you will never be treated with respect while sitting in the back of a Toyota truck.

These are merely guidelines upon which you may improve. Try tossing a martini glass over your shoulder with a carefree laugh.

Remember, if you can get away with doing things an ordinary person would be thrown in jail for, you are well on your way to becoming a Famous Person.